The New Zealand Immigration Guide

by Adam Starchild

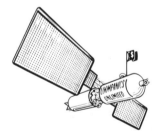

Loompanics Unlimited
Port Townsend, Washington

The New Zealand Immigration Guide

© 1997 by Adam Starchild

Published by:
Loompanics Unlimited
PO Box 1197
Port Townsend, WA 98368

Loompanics Unlimited is a division of Loompanics Enterprises, Inc.
1-360-385-2230

Cover artwork by Terry LaBan
Bird and animal illustrations by David Hartz

ISBN 1-55950-154-5
Library of Congress Card Catalog 97-71601

Contents

NEW ZEALAND

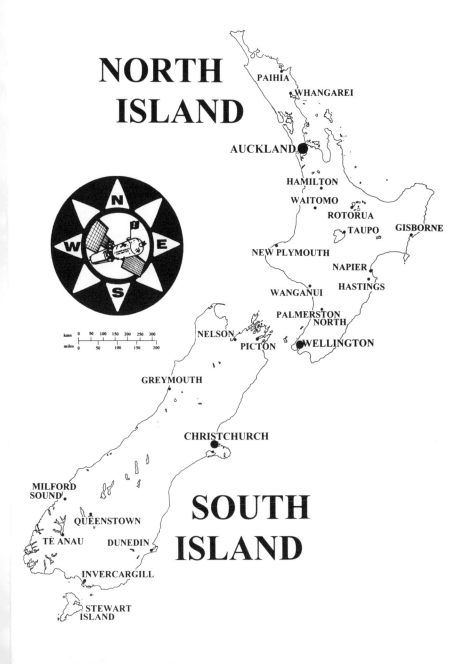

NORTH
ISLAND

PAIHIA

WHANGAREI

AUCKLAND

HAMILTON

WAITOMO

ROTORUA

TAUPO

GISBORNE

NEW PLYMOUTH

NAPIER

HASTINGS

WANGANUI

PALMERSTON
NORTH

NELSON

PICTON

WELLINGTON

GREYMOUTH

CHRISTCHURCH

MILFORD
SOUND

SOUTH
ISLAND

QUEENSTOWN

TE ANAU

DUNEDIN

INVERCARGILL

STEWART
ISLAND

kms 0 50 100 150 200 250 300
miles 0   50   100   150   200

Chapter One
Land of the Kiwis
— An Overview

Kiwis, as New Zealanders like to call themselves, live in one of the most unique places on earth. Composed of two main islands, North Island and South Island, and several smaller islands, New Zealand is a land of wonder and opportunity. With an area of about 268,000 square kilometers, New Zealand boasts golden beaches, lakes, volcanoes, ancient forests, snow-capped mountains, glaciers, fiords, and large modern cities. Consider that New Zealand is roughly the same size as the British Isles and you can understand the great diversity that the land of the Kiwis offers.

New Zealand is located in the South Pacific Ocean, southeast of Australia. It is a self-governing country, and a member of the Commonwealth of Nations.

A generally mountainous country, more than 60% of New Zealand lies between 200 and 1,070 meters above sea level, and more than 200 mountains exceed elevations of 2,200 meters. Running almost the entire length of the South Island is a massive mountain chain referred to as the Southern Alps. Plains interspersed between mountains can provide breathtaking sights.

Lying in the Temperate Zone, much of New Zealand's climate is mild. Overall, the climate can be described as being warm in the summer, and mild and wet in the winter. The differences between seasons don't vary much, although there can be wide differences because of elevation. For example, the average temperature at Auckland, on the North Island, ranges between 19 degrees C (66.2

degrees F) in January and 10.6 degrees C (51 degrees F) in July. Remember that because New Zealand lies south of the equator, its seasons are reversed in comparison to the seasons north of the equator. In general, the farther south you go, the cooler temperatures become. Throughout much of the islands, rainfall averages are moderate to abundant.

New Zealand's most important natural resource is its land, which is excellent for farming, dairies, and sheep raising. Forests are also an important resource. The islands have mineral deposits as well, including coal, gold, limestone, sand, gravel, dolomite, and magnesite. Natural gas can be found on the North Island and off the island's southwest coast.

Most of New Zealand's population of approximately 3.3 million people live in modern cities. Auckland on the North Island is the largest city, with more than 850,000 residents. At the southern tip of the North Island is Wellington, the capital city, with about 325,000 people, while Christchurch, with a population of slightly over 300,000, is the largest city of the South Island. New Zealand's cities are bustling centers of activity with busy streets, shopping centers, and office buildings.

Over the last several years, the trend toward urbanization has increased. Whereas in the latter part of the 19th century, close to 75% of New Zealanders lived in rural areas, today that figure has dropped to 15%. Although agriculture remains an important part of New Zealand's economy, commerce and manufacturing have taken on an ever-increasing role.

New Zealand is a vital, progressive country where enterprise and new ideas pay off handsomely. One of its great strengths is how small, innovative companies meet the needs of their customers through quick diversification. If there is one thing the business sector needs, it is experienced managers and equity capital. People with management expertise, who can start a business or offer their experience to existing companies, or who can provide valuable consulting services, are in demand. For many people, New Zealand is a land of opportunity.

Recognizing the value of new blood, New Zealand's immigration legislation and policies toward newcomers have been revised. The philosophy is that New Zealand is a growing country, and immigrants should be able to contribute to and enjoy that growth. To this end, the new legislation requires that people considering moving to New Zealand must have the experience and assets to establish themselves. The social well-being of the country is a major consideration.

Of course, these immigration policies are also designed to result in social benefits. The government encourages migrants from more countries than in the past, as it hopes to achieve a balanced mix of immigrants that will enhance the country's cultural milieu.

Although it is a small country, New Zealand is known around the world for its clean environment, its picturesque beauty, and fine lifestyle. Indeed, hundreds of thousands of people visit the country each year to enjoy the high standards of living, friendly people, and open roads. Many of these people decide to apply for permanent resident status, making New Zealand their home.

Those coming to New Zealand for the first time are met by a pristine land that borders on paradise. The cleanness of the air is most striking. Not only does it smell clean, but it looks clean, providing sharper images at greater distances than newcomers are accustomed to.

Newcomers are also struck by the lushness of the islands. Forests are thick and full, vital with life. Farms are abundant with crops and livestock, and the whole land seems to thrive.

The land itself is vibrant, for it is a relatively young land, a country thrust up from the ocean floor a scant five million years ago. Given that the earth itself was formed some 4½ billion years ago, New Zealand is a geological infant.

There is no other place in the world like New Zealand. The islands are a land of mountains and plains, glaciers, fiords, woodlands and great ancient forests. New Zealand is a place of kiwifruit plantations, sheep farmers and dairies, and also cosmopolitan cities. It is a place of clean rivers and lakes, snow-capped peaks, and is surrounded by ocean and air that are pure and fresh. It is, in the words of many visitors, as well as those who come to stay, truly a wonderland, perhaps the last on earth.

When noted on a world map, New Zealand appears to be a small, insignificant group of islands. Bordered by the South Pacific Ocean on the east and the Tasman Sea on the west, one might simply glance over it. But to do so would be to overlook one of the world's most desirable countries in which to live.

In the following pages, you'll find out why so many people have decided to move to New Zealand. They have found that it's truly one of the finest places on earth, and that opportunity abounds for those willing to build upon their dreams.

Mt. Cook

Chapter Two
A Geographical Perspective

Inhabiting a nation made up of islands, few New Zealanders live far from the sea. The ocean and its relative isolation from other land masses have played a large part in shaping both the physical features and nature of the country. In many respects, New Zealand is unlike anywhere else.

New Zealand is a tiny remnant of a once vast super-continent called Gondwanaland. Australia, Antarctica, India, Africa, and South America were also part of this immense, ancient land mass. New Zealand has been formed over 550 million years as a result of the shifting and colliding of great plates that underlie the earth's crust. Some 80 million years ago, the land that came to be known as New Zealand parted from Antarctica and Australia. From that time until about five million years ago, New Zealand was changed often by the sea, the land rising and falling, being divided only to be reunited. This continued until a major uplifting created the North and South Islands, which have changed little since then. However, as the crustal plates of the earth continue to move, the uplift proceeds, causing the Southern Alps to creep slowly higher at the rate of a fraction of an inch a year.

Because much of its land area was formed about five million years ago, a relatively short period in geologic time, New Zealand has little in common with Australia, its closest neighbor. Thus New Zealand has evolved independently.

Mt. Ruapehu and the Desert Road (North Island)

While New Zealand is made up of several islands, two, the North Island and the South Island, are the biggest and most important. Most New Zealanders live on these two islands, which are also the home of most of the nation's economic activity. The two islands, both of which are relatively narrow, run in a roughly north-south direction. They have much in common, but also possess many distinctive features.

The North Island

Of the two major islands, the North Island has a more irregular coastline than that of the South Island. This is especially true around its northern coast. Along the east coast lie the major mountains of the North Island. In the north central region is a volcanic range with active volcanoes—Mt. Ruapehu, 2,797 meters, or about 9,175 feet in elevation and the highest point on the North Island; Mt. Ngauruhoe, 2,291 meters or about 7,515 feet high; and Tongariro, 1,968 meters or about 6,458 feet high.

The North Island also has several rivers, most of which begin in the east and central mountains. Of these, the Waikato River is the longest in New Zealand at 434 kilometers or about 270 miles.

The North Island is a bit warmer and drier than the South Island. Still, the highest mountain peaks retain snow throughout the year.

For Mountains, Glaciers and Lakes — Head South

Mt. Cook and the Hooker Glacier.

The South Island is home to the Southern Alps, an impressive mountain chain that extends for almost the entire length of the island in a southwest to northeast direction. The range is dotted by 17 peaks that exceed 3,048 meters, or about 10,000 feet, in elevation. The highest point of the range, about at the middle of the range, is Mt. Cook at 3,764 meters, or about 12,349 feet.

A number of spectacular glaciers are also found throughout the Southern Alps. Two of the greatest, the Fox and Franz Josef, are quite accessible and provide scenery that is little short of remarkable. Glaciers of the past have left their marks on gouged valleys, moraines, and deep lakes. Although the North Island has the magnificent Lake Taupo, the South Island boasts a variety of lakes, which are sustained by the glaciers and the snowpacks of the mountains.

The South Island also contains large tracts of rich plains that are used for agriculture. Many of these plains contain fertile alluvial soil that has been deposited by rivers over time. In the South Canterbury region, gravel plains are used by sheep herders.

Unlike the North Island's jagged coastline, the coast of the South Island is somewhat more regular, but still has its share of rocky cliffs, caves, and beaches of rough surf. Seals can often be found sunning themselves on the beaches. Cutting into the coast along the southwest corner of the South Island are several fiords. On the whole, the South Island's coast, despite being less jagged than that of the North Island's, is the more rugged of the two islands. Its beaches are pounded by heavy surf and winds, big rocks stand like guards on the sand, and the water is cool, especially the farther south you travel.

The Weather

New Zealand's clean air and mild climate are very much a result of its geography. Located in the southern hemisphere, New Zealand's weather is affected by weather patterns that originate over Antarctica. These patterns would be expected to bring cold, unsettled air, but New Zealand's great mountain chains block the potentially brutal cold, filtering it and in the process producing a favorable climate known for its moderate temperatures, steady rainfall, and pleasant skies.

Still, you must remember that much of New Zealand is mountainous and the weather in the mountains can at times be severe. Since the islands stretch in a relatively north-south direction, and the prevailing winds run west to east, most weather systems strike the mountains first, particularly the Southern Alps. In the mountains, gale force winds, heavy rain, and snow can blow in during any season, even summer.

Although the other areas of New Zealand may also experience various types of weather, the variations are not nearly so harsh. On the North Island, Auckland's average temperature throughout the year, for example, varies less than 10 degrees C (19 degrees C in summer and 10 degrees C in winter). While the average annual temperatures of places on the South Island tend to be a bit lower, they don't vary much either. Queenstown on the South Island has an average temperature in summer of 22 degrees C and an average winter temperature of 8 degrees C, a variation of 14 degrees. Most areas of the islands experience moderate amounts of rainfall.

On the whole, New Zealand's climate is considered to be maritime. As such, it is generally mild, with plenty of sunshine, moderate to abundant rainfall, and few extremes of temperature. Because of the mountains, there is much variation; yet there is also much in the weather that can be counted on. Many New Zealanders are able to swim in the ocean for more than half of the year. The overall mild climate also results in a year-long growing season in many parts of the country.

New Zealand further benefits from global weather patterns that spare it much of the air from the northern hemisphere. Thus, the islands have little worry over the pollution from the north, for it never reaches them. Because much of the island nation's winds originate over or near Antarctica, the air is exceedingly clean. There is virtually no air pollution near the South Pole, and none for the winds to blow to New Zealand.

Vegetation

Because New Zealand separated from other land masses some 80 million years ago, many individual species of plants have originated in the country. Before people arrived, the country was covered with thick forests and heavy undergrowth, which provided the habitat for a variety of native animals.

Although the arrival of settlers resulted in the destruction of many of the original forests, the forests that remain are full and lush. Ferns are a predominate species. Some tree ferns grow up to 15 meters high. The forest floor is covered with a variety of smaller ferns, mosses, and lichens. The canopy of the forest, called the "bush" by the Kiwis, is often a web of numerous creepers, palm lilies, and ferns.

Square Kauri pine tree (note the size of the car).

While ferns may be found just about everywhere, and generally provide the distinctive character of a New Zealand forest, the country has several other species of trees, more than a hundred in fact. On the North Island, a few kauri pine forests thrive. Able to grow more than 50 meters high, these pines typically lose their lower branches, standing like long telephone poles with thick, bushy tops.

New Zealand has many varieties of flowers. Orchids can be found in many locations, in numerous tints and shades. Close to 60 different species can be found in the forests. Because they can provide a multiple of hues, orchids are a favorite choice of gardeners, who use them to add color to their gardens.

Flowers adorn the mountains as well. About 500 species of flowering plants, found only in New Zealand, provide a tapestry to alpine areas. One of the most common of these plants is the white mountain daisy. Another is the Mount Cook Lily.

The varied species of New Zealand's flowers enhance the landscape, as well as parks. Indeed, it is often suggested to visitors that they see the parks that can be found in most of New Zealand's cities to observe for themselves some of the flowery beauty that is New Zealand.

The Animal Life

Like its vegetation, whose evolution was influenced by New Zealand's geography, the country's animal life was also affected. Humans did not arrive until around 800 A.D. Before them, the only mammals native to New Zealand were bats. Biologists believe that one species of bat has no close relatives anywhere else, while another is likely to have come from Australia. Frogs, lizards, and the tuatara are other common land animals. Often referred to as a living fossil, the tuatara, a lizardlike creature, is one of the world's most ancient reptiles and can be traced back to a time before the dinosaurs. It survives on the offshore islands.

Birds provide New Zealand with some of the country's most interesting creatures. New Zealand possesses an assortment of flightless birds. Without the presence of predatory species of mammals, birds did not need to fly and many species became flightless. Because of an abundant food supply, many also became rather plump. One of the most well-known of the flightless birds is the kiwi, which has, in the minds of some people, become associated with New Zealand. Of course, other birds do fly, but some researchers believe they may have flown to New Zealand, or been blown here from other lands. Among the many native species of bird are songbirds, including the bellbird and tui. Indeed New Zealand has a rather large population of wild birds, of which 23 kinds are native to the islands. There are also many seabirds and species of birds that migrate, stopping at the islands during certain times of the year.

The tuatara (Sphenodon punctatum).

The noble kiwi (Apterygiformes), *national bird of New Zealand.*

The bellbird (Anthornis melanura), *one of
New Zealand's most-loved songbirds.*

The parson bird (Prosthemadera novaeseelandiae),
famed for its powers of mimicry.

When humans came to New Zealand, they brought with them their animals. The Polynesians were likely the ones to introduce the rat and dog, as well as food plants like the yam. The Europeans brought birds, cattle, sheep, and also deer, opossums, rabbits, and goats. Europeans also brought many plants, including deciduous trees and those for crops.

Life in New Zealand Waters

The ocean waters surrounding New Zealand teem with many kinds of fish. Among the most well-known are snappers, blue cod, flounder, swordfish, and shark. Common shellfish include mussels and oysters. Whales and seals are also abundant in the seas around the islands.

It is not only the ocean, however, that provides edible fish to New Zealanders. In the freshwater lakes and rivers, whitebait, eel, and lampreys abound. Trout and salmon, which have been imported, are also found in large numbers.

A Unique Land

Because it has been isolated from other land masses for such a long time, New Zealand has been able to evolve quite independently. Its unique evolution has resulted in islands that are spectacular in their individuality.

Unlike many other countries that are saddled with overpopulation, pollution, environmental degradation, and the deteriorating lifestyle that such conditions always bring, New Zealand is a young land with great promise and potential. Its pristine environment, magnificent scenery and natural wonders combine to make it one of the most desirable countries in the world.

Chapter Three
The History of New Zealand

Until about 800 A.D. New Zealand had no human inhabitants. The first people to come to the islands were Polynesians. These early settlers traveled to the islands by sea, probably from Tahiti, in large seaworthy canoes. Having spread through the South Pacific for several thousand years, the Polynesians had acquired excellent skills in sailing and navigation. Their arrival at New Zealand was inevitable.

When they arrived, they found that New Zealand was unlike any other land they had previously found and settled. It was larger, had cooler and more varied weather patterns, possessed a temperate rather than tropical climate, and had far more geographic features than

Maori chief wearing a feather headdress.

16

the Polynesians were used to. It took some time for them to adapt to this new home.

Eventually, however, a distinctive culture arose. Known today as the Maori, the first settlers were the ancestors to a people who developed customs and traditions that boasted fine art, a rich mythology, and a complex social structure. They also came to understand and appreciate their new environment.

This "valuing" of the land became a focal point of Maori culture. Even today the Maori are sometimes referred to as the "Tangata Whenua," or "People of the Land," an appellation that occupies a place of special status in New Zealand.

It is said that a people, the Moriori, about whom little is known, had already settled on the eastern coast of the North Island prior to the arrival of the first immigration wave of Polynesians, but hardly any evidence remains of this event. According to the oral histories that have been handed down, the Moriori were absorbed by the Polynesian settlers, with the remainder driven out and eventually settling on the Chatham Islands.

Once the immigration started, the Polynesians quickly spread along the coasts and rivers of both the North and South Islands. It was the North Island that retained the greatest population.

The society that the Maori developed on New Zealand was a stratified one. Children were born into "chiefly" or noble families (rangatira), or they were born as commoners (tutua). During war, captured enemies were made slaves.

Elders, the family heads, provided authority. The Maori did not have towns, but instead lived in "communities." These might be just a few houses to more than 500 dwellings that would comprise a village. The rangatira families provided the authority for the village. In times of conflict, or when the need arose to forge area-wide trade pacts, villages and tribes would unite under a single leader called an ariki.

Much of the life in Maori settlements was communal. The residents of settlements worked together in growing and gathering food, and also defense. When shortages of food occurred, the supplies would be conserved so that all could share in what was still available.

The Coming of the Europeans

In 1642, the Dutch seafarer and navigator Abel Janszoon Tasman, with two ships *(Heemskerck* and *Zeehaen)* spotted what would come to be known as the Southern Alps of South Island. He sailed northward around the future Cape Farewell, and dropped anchor in what is now called Golden Bay.

When a Maori canoe rammed a small boat that was traveling from the *Zeehaen* to the *Heemskerck*, fighting broke out, resulting in both Maori and Dutch casualties. Naming the spot "Murderers' Bay," Tasman sailed northward up the coast of North Island and departed the area, leaving a

Abel Janszoon Tasman, first European to visit New Zealand.

legacy of a wavy line labeled "Staten Landt" (the Dutch name for South America) on the nautical chart. European cartographers of the time thought that Tasman's markings might indicate the western edge of a great southern continent. Within a few years they realized that this was not so, and changed the name to "Nieuw Zeeland."

It wasn't until 1769 that European adventurers revisited the islands. British naval officer and explorer Captain James Cook arrived at the same time as a Frenchman, De Surville, although neither was aware of the other's presence, as they were on opposite sides of the islands. Cook circumnavigated the two major islands, and also clashed with the Maori. He took possession of the islands for Great Britain, although his claim wasn't recognized by the government for 75 years.

Captain James Cook

Cook returned twice to New Zealand, his last voyage taking place in 1779. He established harmonious relations with the Maori, and Cook and naturalist Joseph Banks studied and wrote about Maori life and culture. Cook's journal, *A Voyage Towards the South Pole and Round the World,* was published in 1777. It brought the knowledge of New Zealand's many wonders to the Western world.

For quite some time, Europeans showed little interest in New Zealand. After all, they had the Americas, India, Africa, and Australia to colonize, and New Zealand provided interest only for explorers who were curious about the unusual plants and animals the islands offered.

In time, though, facts about New Zealand's uniqueness and its resources became common knowledge among seafarers and explorers, particularly those who sailed the South Pacific, and by the early 1800s European commercial interests were beginning operations on the islands. British and American whalers found the populations of whales and seals to be plentiful, and the British quickly realized that kauri forests provided excellent wood for sailing ships. Such resources promised profits, and more men began voyaging to New Zealand. Families soon followed, along with missionaries, merchants and traders, and it wasn't long before settlements were established.

The first settlements were built among the Bay of Islands on the North Island. By 1840, under the management of the New Zealand Company, major efforts at immigration began and the whole of New Zealand was opening up.

The Treaty of Waitangi

Since the Maori were already inhabitants of New Zealand, England sent Captain William Hobson to the islands to negotiate a treaty with the Maori chieftains. He forged the Treaty of Waitangi in 1840 and signed it with 50 of the chieftains. The treaty took its name after the place in the Bay of Islands where it was signed.

This was not a treaty of conquest. In exchange for sovereignty of the islands of New Zealand, England agreed to respect the land ownership rights of the Maori. The Maori in turn placed themselves under the protection of the British government and became subjects of Queen Victoria. To protect the Maori from exploitation — the kind that had happened in other areas of the world where the Europeans had colonized — the Maori had the right to sell their land, but only through the Crown.

Maoris hunting the now-extinct moa bird.

The treaty resulted in a flood of immigration, from England, as well as Scotland, Scandinavia, and France. Drawn by New Zealand's magnificent landscape, its resources (gold, for example, was discovered in 1865), and the chance to start a new life, colonists streamed into the country. Many were ignorant of the spirit and language of the Treaty of Waitangi, however, and merely took what they wished.

Such actions led to tensions over land, which resulted in uprisings and wars, notably in 1845 and 1848, and between 1860 and 1870. After 1881 the colonial government adopted policies that established a permanent peace between the Maori and the settlers.

From then on, the Europeans and Maori have worked together to create a modern New Zealand. Through the end of the 19th century, and the beginning of the 20th, immigration increased. These periods saw extensive immigration from England. During the 19th century, Chinese people also came to New Zealand in large numbers, particularly during the times of the gold rushes.

After World War II, and up through the late 1960s, the Dutch, as well as many people from Eastern Europe, arrived. Many of those who arrived right after the war came to start new lives, for they had lost everything during the conflict.

Today, with the improved air links that connect New Zealand with other countries around the world, immigration continues. Those who come to New Zealand often share many of the same motivations. They come because of the opportunities and beautiful environment that New Zealand offers; they come to fulfill their dreams of a new life.

New Zealand's Government

A parliamentary form of government was established in New Zealand in 1856. For most of the 19th century, liberal and conservative elements alternated in power, although much of the political thought of the time was largely progressive. Universal male suffrage and compulsory education were instituted relatively early in the country's history. This progressive attitude continues today.

Toward the end of the 19th century, the government pursued a program of land reform in which large, speculative land holdings were acquired by the government, which then divided them and made them available for purchase by small landowners. Another progressive idea included the establishment of a minimum rate of pay, and still another focused on women's suffrage. Indeed, in 1893 New Zealand became the first country to grant women the right to vote.

New Zealand was made a dominion in 1907, but its government remained the same. During the world wars, New Zealand fought on the side of the Allies. Its ties to Britain remain strong.

Today, New Zealand is a type of monarchy. The British monarch holds the title of the King or Queen of New Zealand, but the country is independent and democratic. The monarchy's representative is the Governor-General, whose powers are statutory. New Zealand has a unicameral Parliament, which is known as the House of Representatives. In 1950, a second house, which was known as the Legislative Council, was abolished. The members of the House of Representatives, also referred to as members of Parliament, are elected and serve for three-year terms.

It is the task of Parliament to enact laws and oversee the running of the government. Parliament wields power through its control of money. The government can raise or spend money only with the approval of Parliament.

The Prime Minister is usually the leader of the party with the most members elected to the Parliament. He recommends to the Governor-General who should serve as ministers in the government. The ministers are then responsible for many of the government's operations.

Citizens or permanent residents over the age of 18 have the right to vote. In addition, they must have lived continuously in New Zealand for at least a year at some time, and they must have lived at least one month in the place in which they are voting.

Locally, New Zealand is divided into 104 counties. The exception here is some of the small offshore islands which do not belong to any county. In areas of high population, local government is managed by cities, boroughs or towns. Where population is small and scattered, local government falls to the counties themselves.

In recent years, New Zealand's politics have been dominated by two parties: The National Party and the Labour Party. Occasionally, individuals have left the major parties and been elected to Parliament as independents. There are also candidates of minor parties.

The Emergence of a National Identity

In 1907, New Zealand's colonial status ended, and in 1947 all legislative connections to Great Britain were cut. While it remains a member of the British Commonwealth of Nations, New Zealand is entirely independent.

The sense of a national identity has been evolving throughout the 20th century. This was especially noticeable when New Zealand's artists and authors began to break with mainstream British art and literature. By the 1930s, distinctive New Zealand art and literature began to flourish.

It was also at about this time that New Zealanders began to think of themselves as New Zealanders. Second- and third-generation offspring of the original immigrants knew no home except New Zealand. The many cultures of the various people that made up New Zealand also began to merge, accelerating a process that had begun during the early days of colonization. Widespread inter-marriage between people of the various cultures that came together in the country hastened the emergence of a national identity. Many of the people who identify themselves as Maori are, in fact, people of mixed blood, sharing both Maori and European traits. Many New Zealanders don't even bother to identify themselves according to race; they are simply New Zealanders.

24

The mixing of ancestry promoted the mixing of cultures and traditions. In time, a distinctive New Zealand culture arose. That culture has resulted in several prominent features. New Zealanders tend to share a strong sense of social justice; they believe in hard work and that their country is a place of opportunity; they respect and appreciate the environment; and they are proud of New Zealand's institutions, social progress, and heritage.

The trend toward a single culture that is a synthesis of the many cultures that immigrants brought to New Zealand is likely to accelerate. As the world moves into the 21st century, it is probable that New Zealand will continue to evolve, building on the strengths that it has forged in the past. Clearly, New Zealand will emerge as a model for the rest of the world, for it is a country where people from various backgrounds have come together to create a new land.

Chapter Four
The Kiwis —
New Zealand's People

Despite being a small country, New Zealand is far from being tightly populated. There is plenty of room for more immigrants.

Of the total population of roughly 3.3 million, most live in modern, urban areas. In fact, more than 2 million New Zealanders live in or near urban areas, and more than 85% live in communities of at least a thousand people. Auckland, on the North Island, is the largest city in the country with more than 850,000 people. Wellington, the capital on the southern tip of the North Island, has a population of about 325,000. The South Island's largest city, Christchurch, has slightly over 300,000 residents.

The country is not densely populated, with just over 10 people per square kilometer. Only Australia, Canada, and Argentina have fewer people in an equal area.

The North Island has the greater population of the two main islands, with about 2.5 million people. The South Island is home to slightly under 900,000.

Of the total population, just over 80% of New Zealanders are descended from Europeans, about 10% are Maori, 3% are Polynesian (who arrived after the Europeans and are not grouped with the Maori), with smaller numbers of Chinese, Indian, Dutch, and French, and an assortment of other groups as well. Together, these various ethnic groups have created an independent and vigorous culture that is neither wholly Western nor Polynesian. Indeed, New Zealand has become a Kiwi Melting Pot.

26

A Thoroughly Modern Lifestyle

Most New Zealanders have easy access to thousands of goods and services. For the majority, shopping entails a short walk or drive to a supermarket, shopping center, local shop, or convenience store, called a dairy. Dairies carry such products as milk (obviously), breads, and other items that people need but may not wish to go to a larger store to purchase. There are even some stores that remain open around the clock.

Other stores, including modern supermarkets, are usually found in various locations, making it easy for New Zealanders to buy whatever they need. Specialty shops, selling just about everything, abound. Fast-food outlets are also growing in popularity. New Zealanders can choose from such chains as McDonalds, Pizza Hut, KFC, and many local fish and chip establishments.

Unlike the shopping centers and stores in many other countries, New Zealand stores are designed to facilitate shoppers. Most provide plenty of room and are located so that traffic is kept to a minimum, making shopping more enjoyable and relaxing.

For those New Zealanders who live within the parameters of major towns and cities (even those who still work the farms are not far from such centers, however), a modern, cosmopolitan lifestyle is taken for granted.

As late as the early 1960s, there were few restaurants that were not inside a hotel. Today, hundreds of restaurants, specializing in various ethnic dishes, are found throughout the cities.

As late as the early 1980s, many stores would close down from Friday night through Monday morning. Today, most stores remain open for business through Saturday, and many stay open on Sundays, too. New Zealanders enjoy all of the comforts and luxuries that the people in any advanced Western society take for granted.

New Zealanders also realize that their country can compete with the best countries of the world in world markets. Consequently, New Zealand is becoming a major player in the global economy, especially in the Pacific. The more the ties that had bound New Zealand to Britain are cut, the greater is New Zealand's thrust into world trade. Even as trade with Australia, New Zealand's long-time traditional partner, has grown, so has it grown with the United States. In many ways, New Zealand's trade with the U.S. is more important than its trade with Europe. Other important trading partners include Hong Kong, Singapore, Japan, and other countries of the Pacific.

As New Zealand's influence expands across the Pacific, and, indeed, around the world, New Zealanders are increasingly gaining importance in the sciences, arts, and entertainment. Around the Pacific rim, New Zealand entertainers are in demand, and in the business world and international politics, New Zealanders are gaining prominence.

Without question, New Zealand is a land growing in importance. Clearly, it is one of the new lands of opportunity.

There's No Place Like Home

In selecting a home, New Zealanders have the option of living in the city, the suburbs, or a rural area. Moreover, they can pick a mountain retreat or a home along the coast. Because the country has a low population density, there is ample room for housing, and New Zealanders have far more choices than many other people.

Many New Zealanders live in a house that has three or four bedrooms. It will likely have a kitchen, dining room, and a room for relaxing (often called a lounge). The lot sizes vary, depending whether the home is in the city or the suburbs, but suburban lots are much like suburban lots in the United States. On days off you will likely see people tending to their yards and maintaining the upkeep of their homes. Of course, there are also professional services that will maintain yards and homes, just as there are in other advanced countries.

Real estate agents are available to help residents as well as newcomers to New Zealand in purchasing the home that fits their needs and lifestyle. Homes are available with many extras, including swimming pools, Jacuzzis, even tennis courts. The prices vary, depending on the type of house and location. The average home costs slightly over $NZ 200,000 (or about 130,000 U.S. dollars). Upscale homes typically run between $300,000 and $500,000.

One of the most popular cities to settle in is Auckland. Residents in all areas of Auckland (and this is true of most of New Zealand) have access to good schools, shopping centers, business establishments, restaurants, and parks.

The prices of homes vary greatly as one leaves Auckland. In Wellington, the average home costs close to $180,000, while on the South Island prices for homes in Christchurch average slightly over $125,000.

In recent years high-rise apartment buildings and townhouses have grown in popularity. Many of these are built on waterfront or other scenic areas.

Health Care

In many respects, the quality of life within a country is reflected in its health care system. Whereas many of the world's most powerful countries grapple with health care systems that are out of control — just consider the major efforts underway in the United States to reform its health care system — everyone in New Zealand enjoys medical coverage. Everyone has access to hospital treatment, and visits to the doctor are subsidized by the government depending on income. Prescription drugs are also subsidized, although there is a co-payment by the patient.

For New Zealanders who buy supplementary health insurance, various plans are available. A family of four, for example, can receive about 80% of their medical costs for less than $400 a year (U.S. equivalent funds). If that same family of four opts to purchase a policy that will cover all of their medical bills, it will cost them less than $100 per month (again U.S. equivalent funds).

Compare that to health care costs in the United States where it is not uncommon to pay up to $5,000 per year for health insurance, and the insured may still have to pay deductibles every time he or she goes to the doctor.

New Zealanders also have a wide choice of treatment options. They may select treatment at a variety of private, public, or voluntary health organizations.

Unlike many other countries, this high-quality health care is largely paid for through income taxes. Should a New Zealander suffer an accident or be stricken with a disease or life-threatening ailment, he or she will have immediate access to health care.

Along with providing free treatment for disease and accidents, the public sector, for instance, provides treatment for pregnancy, some geriatric conditions, and dental care for children under 18. The private sector provides daily health care through family doctors, dentists, and other health care professionals.

There are both public and private hospitals. While there may be a wait for some types of elective or non-emergency treatment at the public hospitals, there is usually no wait at the private ones. Of course, private hospitals carry greater costs for the patient, but this is where private health insurance of a supplementary nature comes in. More than 50% of New Zealanders subscribe to a health insurance plan, and the number is growing.

On the whole, the quality of New Zealand's health care system is high. Doctors understand the latest treatments and hospitals offer the latest in medical technology. Health care is accessible to everyone, and there are various supplemental plans from which to choose.

New Zealanders at Play

Every March "The Round-the-Bays Run" is held in Auckland. Up to 80,000 joggers participate in the 10.5 kilometer (6.5 mile) course that winds its way from Victoria Park along the waterfront to Saint Heliers Bay. No other athletic event anywhere in the world has as many participants.

The Round-the-Bays Run is symbolic of New Zealanders' fitness-consciousness and love of sports. Many New Zealanders are passionate about their sports, and sports occupy a high level of prestige in the country. Sports champions are idolized by young and old alike. Cricket, rugby, squash, jogging, and sailing are some of the most popular sports, followed closely by skiing, fishing, mountaineering, tennis, golf, and hunting. It is not uncommon to see groups of friends playing casual games of various sports in parks or open fields.

Golf is becoming a world-class sport in New Zealand. Not only is it played avidly by New Zealanders, but many tourists who visit the country make it a point to play on the nation's superb golf courses.

Horse racing is one of the most popular spectator sports. It is little wonder that New Zealand boasts exceptional racetracks and racecourses, or that New Zealand's thoroughbreds are considered to be some of the finest in the world.

In a nation surrounded by the sea, yachting naturally commands great interest. Yachtsmen from New Zealand have made it to the challengers' finals of the America's Cup; and Peter Blake, a New Zealander, won the Round the World yachting race in 1990.

Unlike some countries in which the land is fenced off with "Private, No Trespassing" signs warning the public to keep out, much of New Zealand is open to everyone. Vast tracts of pristine countryside have been reserved by the government for the public, allowing New Zealanders access to the coast, rivers, mountains, and forests.

New Zealand has, in fact, become an excellent place for alpine hunting, to which hunters are drawn by the lure of thar and chamois. Wild pigs and goats, as well as smaller game, can be found in the bush country.

Fishing is another major pastime. Ocean fishermen have their choice of prime spots. One of the best is around the Bay of Islands, off the North Island. Freshwater fishermen find that rainbow and brook trout will offer them superior sport at various lakes and rivers.

Skiers aren't disappointed in New Zealand either. On the North Island, the best skiing can be found at Mt. Ruapehu, although other sites offer conditions almost as good. On the South Island skiers have their choice of slopes when traveling from Queenstown and Wanaka.

New Zealand is a land devoted to sports. Many of its people play as often as they watch.

New Zealanders enjoy all the advantages of modern, technologically advanced countries like the United States, Great Britain, Germany, France, and Japan, but without the problems those countries also must cope with. Many new immigrants choose New Zealand because of its excellent living standards, and lack of noise and pollution.

Most New Zealanders would agree with that assessment. But they would add something more. Overall, New Zealand's people are friendly, and open to new ideas.

Chapter Five
Close-up:
The North Island

While New Zealand is actually made up of several islands, it is the North and South Islands that come to mind when people think of New Zealand. About equal in area, the North Island has the greater population (about 2.5 million to 900,000 people), and it has New Zealand's largest city, Auckland. Cook Strait separates the two islands.

The North Island can be divided into several major regions:

Northland	Auckland
Coromandel Peninsula	The Volcanic Plateau
Bay of Plenty	Waikato
Taranaki	The East Coast
Manawatu and Wanganui	Wellington
Wairarapa	

Each region has its own distinctive features, while sharing the best of what New Zealand offers.

Northland

The Northland, located at the northernmost tip of the North Island, is an area that is married to the sea. Land and ocean are intertwined like lovers by means of numerous bays and harbors.

North Island

Northland

Auckland Region

Coromandel Peninsula

Bay of Plenty Region

Waikato

East Coast

Volcanic
Plateau

Taranaki

Manawatu and
Wanganui

Wairarapu

Wellington Region

It was at the Northland that the first Polynesians landed, and later, with the coming of the Europeans, the Treaty of Waitangi was signed at the Bay of Islands. It was also at the Northland that the first European settlements were founded, and from the Northland that people (Polynesians and Europeans) spread throughout New Zealand.

Beach at Northland.

The area's jagged coast was carved during the ice ages, and eroded further by the rising ocean levels after the ice melted. The result: an assortment of harbors, bays, snaking estuaries, and offshore islands. The land is as rugged as the coast with high hills that come close to being mountains.

Because the Northland is so tightly surrounded by the sea, and also because it is the part of New Zealand closest to the equator, the climate is relatively mild, and residents enjoy mostly subtropical weather much of the year. It rains often in winter, but the summers tend to be dry.

The Northland is known for the huge, strong-wood kauri trees. Before the coming of humans, much of the area was covered with immense kauri forests that were surpassed only by California's great sequoias.

The Northland is also known for its "Desert Coast," the area's northwestern coast from Kaitaia to Cape Reinga. The place is also referred to as the Ninety Mile Beach, although the stretch of seemingly endless sand and stark nature is less than 100 kilometers. This part of the coast is as breathtaking as it is desolate. Yet, not far inland are farms whose productivity stand in sharp contrast to the windswept sands.

Most of the residents of the Northland live in the middle regions of the area. The most important city here is Whangarei, while Dargaville is the most important town. Much of the Northland's population is in and around these two places.

Whangarei, by some estimates, is one of New Zealand's fastest growing cities. The reason is easy to find. Industry has sprouted around the city. Oil refining, ship-building, glass-making, engineering, and cement-making are just some of the industries that are helping to transform Whangarei into one of the nation's most bustling population centers.

Still, compared to the rest of New Zealand, the Northland is underpopulated. (This is not to imply that the rest of New Zealand is crowded. As already noted, New Zealand has one of the lowest population densities of any modern, industrialized country.) There is plenty of room for newcomers to this region of picturesque beaches, stunning vegetation, and a mild climate.

Auckland

With a population nearing 1 million, Auckland is home to just under a third of New Zealand's entire population. From its center

Auckland expands to its suburbs so gradually that it is hard for a person to decide where the city ends and the suburbs begin.

Auckland is actually a city and suburb combined. Suburbs stretch out from the city in every direction. Overall, Auckland covers an area of 1,016 square kilometers (378 square miles), and runs 80 kilometers (50 miles) along the coast. Most suburban houses sit on lots of about a quarter of an acre, allowing residents to enjoy all the city has to offer without feeling congested or cramped.

Auckland's climate can be described in one word — pleasant. Year-round Auckland's weather is neither too hot nor too cold; it has ample rainfall but not so much that the city could be considered rainy.

Originally settled by the Maori, Auckland today has one of the greatest concentrations of Polynesians in the world. The city itself is a blending of cultures. While English is the primary language, more than 20 dialects of Polynesian are spoken.

The city indeed has a high culture. Stores, shops, galleries, and theaters can be found throughout the city. Sailing and fishing are prime recreational pursuits.

Beach near Auckland.

Auckland is surrounded by water and the residents revel in it. To the north and east, Auckland is bordered by the Waitemata Harbour, and to the south and west by the Manukau Harbour.

Auckland has the highest number of pleasure craft per population of any city in the world. Nearly 25% of all households own some type of boat, and it is estimated that residents of Auckland own up to 70,000 pleasure boats. One of the great sporting events of the year is the Auckland Anniversary Day Regatta, held each year near the end of January. Up to 1,000 sailboats of all sizes compete in the Waitemata Harbour.

Often referred to as the "Queen City," Auckland enjoys two fine harbours, a coastline punctuated with offshore islands, several excellent beaches for swimming, and all the trappings of a modern cosmopolitan lifestyle. As remarkable as it sounds, more than 100 beaches lie within an hour's drive of the city.

Coromandel Peninsula

Coromandel Peninsula

Along the North Island's east coast lies the Coromandel Peninsula. Much like the Northland in climate and relationship with the sea, Coromandel enjoys abundant sunshine.

Coromandel is east, southeast of Auckland. Near the northern end of the peninsula, particularly on a clear night, the lights of Auckland can be seen across the Hauraki Gulf. Coromandel, however, is quite different than Auckland. Whereas Auckland is modern and bustling, Coromandel is quiet and undeveloped. Life here is slow and unhurried.

Much of Coromandel's history is tied to gold. At the height of the gold rush around the turn of the century, it is estimated that several hundred mines were working. In those days Coromandel's population almost doubled that of Auckland. Once the gold rush was over, the area returned to its slower pace and quiet, leaving a legacy of magnificent colonial architecture that still stands as a stately reminder of the wild and heady days of gold rush fever. Although the gold rush of the past has been long over, it is thought that several billion dollars worth of gold still lie in the region.

East coast of Coromandel Peninsula.

Bay of Plenty

The shore along the Bay of Plenty is called the "Kiwifruit Coast." In just the last 25 years, kiwifruit has become known around the world; much of it comes from these shores.

The kiwifruit is not native to New Zealand. It comes from the Yangtze Valley of China, and for centuries has been known as the Chinese gooseberry. The original kiwifruit was somewhat smaller and nuttier than today's which has been hybridized into a bigger and sweeter fruit. It is now exported around the world.

The Volcanic Plateau

The Volcanic Plateau is at the heart of New Zealand's North Island. The name of the region fits it well, for here is some of New Zealand's most seismically active land. Although the hot fires that well up from the earth's bowels are still evident in the area, there is also much beauty and bounty.

Built up through eons of volcanic tumult, the plateau sits more than 500 meters above sea level. Volcanic peaks can be found throughout the area; to the north they are lower and either long dormant or extinct, while to the south they are taller and active. Ancient craters have long ago filled with water and become lakes, dotting the landscape between peaks, gorges, and basins.

While perpetually snow-capped Mt. Ruapehu at 2,797 meters is the North Island's highest point, it is the Rotorua area that enjoys celebrity status because of its bubbling mud, exploding geysers, and boiling lava. Rotorua is located in one of the world's most active volcanic zones. Because of its marvelous sights, it is a prime tourist attraction. All around Rotorua are local thermal hot spots that allow viewers a glimpse into the underground energies of the earth.

Rotorua, with a population of around 50,000, is an important center of light industry, forestry, and farming. The city has the greatest concentration of Maori residents in New Zealand and in many ways is the center of Maori culture in the country. Ten lakes throughout the area provide excellent recreation for fishing, swimming, water sports, and pleasure-boating. More than a half-million visitors come to the Rotorua area each year for fun and relaxation.

Even in the region's most capricious places, where the earth's thermal forces are always at work, New Zealanders have found ways to enjoy the marvels nature has offered them. Some of New Zealand's most popular skiing is on the slopes around Mt. Ruapehu. Snow melt feeds surrounding rivers with fresh water that is the home to rainbow and brown trout, providing excellent fishing. For those who wish to witness the earth's underground power, they merely need to trek along one of the many trails that wind in and around the plateau's mountains.

Before man came, the region of the Volcanic Plateau was wild and untamed. Most of the area was covered with scrub and ferns, but today these same places support cities, communities, farms, and pine forests beneath clear blue skies.

Waikato

Along the western coast, in the middle of the North Island, lies Waikato. The mild, wet climate, which throughout the region averages about 50 millimeters (about 44 inches) of rain per year, ensures thick pastures that support numerous dairy herds.

The region is known for its farming and dairy production. While the flatter land is used by dairymen and farmers, who raise fruits and vegetables, as well as stud horses and cattle, the hilly land is used mostly for sheep ranching.

Hamilton is Waikato's capital. It is a prosperous city that has grown up around the Waikato River, and is surrounded by farmland. Hamilton is one of New Zealand's largest cities, and is well-known as an agricultural research center. Located in and around the city are various industries that support agriculture.

The area around Waikato is often referred to as King Country. During the 1860s, much of this land was at the center of a conflict between the British and Maori. Toward the end, the area that a Maori king and his followers held became known as King Country.

Ticket for Waitomo Caves.

At the heart of King Country are the Waitomo Caves, one of New Zealand's most magnificent natural sights. Limestone is one of the most common features of the land here. Limestone is a sedimentary rock, formed on the sea floor over millions of years as the shells and skeletons of small sea creatures are deposited on the ocean bottom. In time, the deposits build up, and, because of the enormous pressure, form a soft rock. As New Zealand rose from the sea, the limestone that had been set down on the sea floor rose, too. As it did, erosion carved huge holes and gaps in the limestone, leaving a surreal landscape filled by high, jagged cliffs, canyons, crags, and caves. Rivers and streams flow in and out of the jumble of rugged rock formations, slowly continuing the work of erosion and reshaping the land.

There seem to be countless kilometers of caves, much of them unexplored. The longest cave, Gardner's Gut, which is near Waitomo Caves, is estimated to have more than eleven kilometers of passages. The caves are like a labyrinth, a puzzle nature has set before man.

Because of its climate, topography, industries, and history, Waikato is distinct from other regions of New Zealand. Like the other regions of the country, it is distinguished by its own character, yet clearly retains the essence of New Zealand.

Taranaki

The region of Taranaki takes its name from the volcano that dominates it. Mount Taranaki (Mount Egmont), whose last major eruption was about two hundred years ago, has shaped the land around it, giving the region an individual identity. The volcano has bestowed fertility on the land, and the region around the mountain overflows with farms.

For years, Taranaki was a region unto itself, self-sufficient and isolated, its people able to derive their needs from the land. Today, however, the region grows and thrives because of the onshore and offshore reserves of natural gas that have been discovered and tapped. Oil has been found, too, and oil rigs have become a common sight on the green fields. All this has brought a prosperity that would have been unimaginable just a few decades ago.

Mount Taranaki is much like an island amid the rest of the region that shares its name. It was the last and largest of the volcanoes that formed the region, and its ecology is distinct. The volcano has evolved without interference from other areas, and thus a variety of unique vegetation and insects have developed around it.

Aware of the volcano's splendor, the government made Taranaki the center of a national park in 1900.

Egmont National Park offers untold beauty to its visitors. In winter, skiers can choose from numerous trails. In summer, the mountain provides a scene from Eden. Streams snake their way down the mountain, and the view from the upper altitudes of the land that stretches below is nothing short of spectacular. Hikers marvel at waterfalls, and breathe deeply of the mountain air.

Manawatu and Wanganui

Along the southwestern coast of the North Island lies the region of the Manawatu and Wanganui rivers. The rivers run through vast flatlands and sandy coastal areas. Farther inland, the country gives way to forests and mountains. Much of the lowlands are covered by grass, though to the south of Levin, gardens and orchards thrive on the warm plains. The climate of the region is a pleasant one, with minor variations throughout the year.

Although it is not one of New Zealand's longest or most rapid-laden rivers, the Wanganui offers breathtaking scenery that few other rivers can match. Perhaps more importantly, it is New Zealand's longest navigable river and it is the Wanganui that gives the region its own special flavor. The Wanganui's source is in the mountains of the interior, and it enriches itself from tributaries that cover over seven thousand square kilometers. The river runs for 290 kilometers, twisting its way through mountains and forests to the Tasman Sea.

From the time of the Maori, the Wanganui provided a route to the interior of the North Island. The European settlers, like the Maori, realizing the river's value to travel and commerce, made channels more navigable and built systems to overcome rapids.

Today, while still serving the interests of commerce, the river provides a marvelous playground for boaters. Jet boaters and canoeists alike enjoy the Wanganui, and various boat trips start out from the city of Wanganui each day.

Elk farming near the Wanganui River.

While the city of Wanganui, with its population of 40,000, is a modern city by any standard, Palmerston North, New Zealand's second largest inland city with a population of 70,000, is the region's biggest metropolitan center.

Although the region of Manawatu and Wanganui is not the first that usually comes to mind when people, especially visitors, think of New Zealand, the area is admired for its tranquil atmosphere and relaxed pace of life. It offers all of the modern amenities that people desire, but without the hectic, stressful trappings that all too often accompany that lifestyle.

The East Coast

The East Coast of the North Island, also known as the Urewera region, is an area of great surf, dense forests, mighty rivers, and clear, crystal lakes. The region begins at the Bay of Plenty on the north and stretches to Hawke's Bay on the south. Much of the region is sparsely populated.

The climate along the coast is mild, and while the coast enjoys moderate rainfall, the interior sections are known for rather high annual rainfall totals. Downpours, especially in the mountains, are not uncommon.

Indeed, much of the region of the East Coast is mountainous. The inland country is dominated by rugged peaks, some of which reach skyward up to 1,500 meters. Along some parts of the coast, Cape Runaway for instance, the mountains meet the sea. Between the mountains lie gorges and hills, many of which have been given over to sheep for grazing. Some of the inland areas are forested, with rivers, waterfalls, and lakes dotting the landscape.

The East Coast is a land of variety. Mountains, swift running rivers, deep canyons, great forests, and pounding surf have combined to give it an individual beauty, even in a country that offers countless natural marvels. The Hawke's Bay region is known as the fruit bowl of New Zealand.

Much of the region's beauty can be found in Urewera National Park. Contained in the park is some of the most spectacular wilderness of the entire North Island.

Wairarapa

Moving southward from Hawke's Bay is the region of Wairarapa. The extreme southern part of the region marks the end of the North Island and the boundary between the North and South Island. The land here alternates between hills and valleys. There are no large mountains in this place of mild climate, light rainfall, and blue skies.

This is sheep land. In the upper part of the Wairarapa, both cattle and sheep graze, while in the lower part of the region the land is used almost exclusively for sheep.

Unlike much of the North Island that is a blend of Maori and European history and culture, the Wairarapa never had a large

Maori population. This region owes most of its modern heritage to the European colonists.

The two major cities of the region, Napier and Hastings, are the centers of a unique architectural heritage. A style known as Art Deco emerged after a devastating earthquake on February 3, 1931. Measuring 7.9 on the Richter scale, the quake rumbled through the northern Wairarapa and Hawke's Bay, causing massive destruction. Rather than permit nature to have its way, however, the residents began rebuilding almost immediately.

Art Deco, distinguished because of its angular forms and optimism, became the dominate architectural style in the area. Today, Napier and Hastings boast Art Deco in its finest representations. In fact, the area in and around Hawke's Bay offers the most concentrated examples of Art Deco of any place in the world.

The northern Wairarapa is not known only for its architecture, however. Napier, with a population of 53,000, is a bustling center of commerce, an important port, and a resort. Although Hastings is often thought of as Napier's twin — its population is about the same — the two cities are quite different. Hastings is inland, whereas Napier lies on the sea, and consequently the commerce of Hastings has to do more with products and services related to the inland area of the Wairarapa.

Despite being different, Napier and Hastings together help to define the northern region of Wairarapa. To the south, it is Wellington that gives the area its character.

Wellington

Wellington, New Zealand's capital, is in many ways unlike any other city in the country. Located on the southern extreme of the North Island, the city is at the midpoint of New Zealand. It is the capital of the country, and a major center for business, culture, and government services.

While many people feel that Wellington's distinctive character is symbolic of New Zealand's overall identity, there are others who feel that Wellington is a city all its own. A cosmopolitan center, Wellington is a harbor to politicians, civil servants, business people, artists, and designers; it is home to many of the brightest and best of the country.

The city is built among hills that seemingly rise up from the sea. The harbor is almost landlocked, yet it is large and the water is fine for navigation. The hills run into mountains that overlook the city and give Wellington an unmatched beauty.

Like most modern capitals, Wellington has developed and expanded in response to the needs of the country. Wellington and the area around it contain over 30% of New Zealand's population. It is a delightful mix of major city and suburb combined. Coexisting side by side are modern neighborhoods with streets that clearly retain their 19th century atmosphere and look. Some well-traveled visitors have likened Wellington to San Francisco, with its co-mingling of architecture both old and new.

The city's growth has been well-planned, however. Roads have been built to minimize congestion, there is plenty of parking within the city, and there are ample walkways for people to move about. Trees and parks enhance the scenery, giving Wellington a pleasant, inviting look.

Without question, Wellington is a growing, vibrant city. It is a place of opportunity. Many corporations maintain their head-quarters in Wellington, making the city a focal point of economic activity. Not surprisingly, major financial and communications networks are also found in the city. Modern transportation systems, its superior deep water port, and rail and road links all combine to ensure Wellington's continued growth.

Much of that growth is supported by Wellington's outstanding educational system. Along with a fine public school system, the city contains a major university, as well as a variety of technical schools and libraries.

The capital of New Zealand has much to offer visitors, as well as those who come to stay. In many ways it provides the very best of New Zealand.

Separating the North Island from the South Island is Cook Strait. The trip, by road/rail ferry, usually lasts about three hours, but once arriving one steps out into an area that is often described as containing a little of all the rest of New Zealand. It is to the south that we now travel.

Ferry crossing Cook Strait between North and South Islands.

Chapter Six
Close-up:
The South Island

The South Island of New Zealand is roughly the size of the North Island, but it is home for only about a third of the country's people. While the North Island can hardly be called densely populated, the South Island has plenty of room for New Zealanders as well as newcomers.

The South Island begins with Nelson on its northern coast and ends at Invercargill on the far south. Stewart Island lies just beyond the Foveaux Strait.

Like the North Island, the South Island can be divided into several major regions:

Nelson	Marlborough
The West Coast	Canterbury
Christchurch	Otago
Dunedin	Southland
Stewart Island	

While sharing all the best that is New Zealand, each of these regions has unique features that sets it apart from the others.

South Island

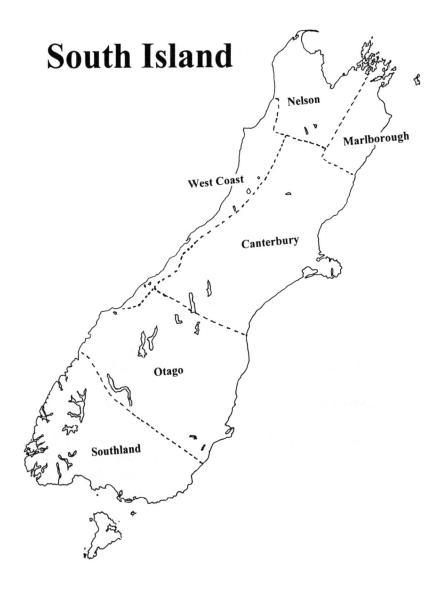

Nelson

Perhaps more than any other region, Nelson seems to share some of all of the others. It is through Nelson that north merges with south. When visiting this northernmost part of the South Island, one can't help but be impressed by the warm coast that is reminiscent of the North Island. Yet, Nelson's mountains are distinctive in their South Island nature. Even the vegetation is in transition. Ferns and trees found mostly on the North Island blend in with southern beech forests, and eventually disappear entirely.

The people of Nelson also find themselves in a transition zone. They live on the South Island, but because of the mountains that isolate them on the northern tip of the island, they tend to look northward rather than to the south.

The climate of Nelson is one of the sunniest in New Zealand. Moderate rainfall and mild temperatures bring forth a bounty of fruits, including kiwifruit, apples, grapes, and avocados. Farms and orchards are spaced over the land, which also contains some of New Zealand's most impressive wilderness and parks.

The city of Nelson, population of about 35,000, is one of New Zealand's oldest cities. It is also one of the quaintest, with some sections retaining an old-country, Victorian look. The city is a prime vacation spot, and the population is said to more than double during every Christmas season.

Having never been linked to the country's rail system, Nelson has developed apart from the rest of New Zealand. This isolation has resulted in Nelson having a distinct atmosphere about it. Over the years it has attracted people who enjoy a quieter style of life, without sacrificing the conveniences of the modern world.

Marlborough

To the east and slightly south of Nelson is Marlborough. Because of their closeness, the two regions have much in common. Yet, there are differences, too, and Marlborough is hardly a Nelson clone. Together with Nelson, Marlborough shares the northern top of the South Island. It also shares New Zealand's sunniest climate. Marlborough, however, has its own geographical features, with a variety of mountains, valleys, and numerous rivers.

Throughout much of the region, sheep grazing and farming are important segments of the economy. Cherries from Marlborough are exported to countries around the world. Although Marlborough has a greater population than Nelson, the region has remained decidedly rural.

Aside from Blenheim and Picton, much of Marlborough is sparsely populated. In some parts of the region, second homes are found in greater abundance than permanent residences. This is hardly surprising, given the region's pleasant temperatures and sunny skies.

The West Coast

The West Coast, often simply referred to as "The Coast," as if no other coast mattered, runs from Karamea in the north to Jackson Bay in the south. The region is about 500 kilometers long and only 50 kilometers wide. It does not have much inland area, but the land it does have away from the coast is mostly mountainous and forested.

Because the region stretches for such a length, its geography varies considerably. As one travels farther south, forests deepen, then, at the upper altitudes, give way to glaciers and dark lakes. Two of the most impressive glaciers are the Franz Josef and the Fox. They creep down the mountains, finding their way through forests and finally stop a few hundred meters above the sea. Their melting ice then merges with a tropical rain forest that spreads beneath its icy edge. Few places in the world offer such stark beauty.

The rain forest along the coast is supported well by a climate that is one of the wettest of New Zealand. Rain is frequent and hard.

Some areas of the Coast average close to 3,000 millimeters (118 inches) of rain a year. It rains an average of 140 days annually.

The West Coast has a history of gold. In the 1860s gold fever drew thousands of prospectors, many of whom eventually settled. It is said that many New Zealanders of today have an ancestor who at one time lived on the West Coast, either as a prospector or settler drawn by the excitement of gold fever and the opportunities that could be found in the gold rush towns.

During those days, numerous towns would rise up and blossom in just weeks around sites of suspected gold. Populations could explode into the thousands, only to fall just as rapidly when the gold field was exhausted. In the late 1860s the population of the West Coast was about 40,000, which is roughly 10,000 more than it is today. Those days of the gold rush were wild and heady, much like America's gold rush, and while little evidence of the boom towns remain, the legacy of the past is a strongly independent population of "Coasters" today.

The Coasters are widely known for being practical, honest, hardy men and women, who are as spirited as they are friendly. They are much like their rugged land.

Canterbury

Canterbury provides a panorama of magnificent topography. Some of New Zealand's greatest stretches of plains, some of its biggest rivers, and some of its most awesome peaks are found in Canterbury. About 300 kilometers long, running north to south, and about 100 kilometers wide, Canterbury is separated from the rest of the South Island by rivers and mountains. It has the largest expanse of flat land in New Zealand.

The plains provide the livelihood for many of the region's inhabitants. Sheep graze on the plains, and Canterbury wool and lamb are exported and prized throughout the world.

The plains also are responsible for the Canterbury nor'wester, a warm, dry wind noted for its bluster and dust-raising power. The wind whips down from the Southern Alps, racing across the flat lands with incessant abandon.

To associate Canterbury only with plains, however, is to diminish the region's many other natural wonders. Along with the vast plains, Canterbury also contains New Zealand's widest rivers and highest mountains. Within those mountains lie extinct volcanoes that once wreaked havoc over the land, their flowing magma laying the foundation of the plains. Today the mountains provide a playground for skiers, who can choose from countless trails and ice-scapes.

Caravan touring the Southern Alps.

Mount Cook National Park contains New Zealand's highest peaks; indeed, this area is one of the most rugged mountain ranges in the world. Part of the Southern Alps, these mountains, in the opinions of many who have visited them as well as the peaks in Switzerland, surpass their European namesake in grandeur.

Seventeen peaks rise above 3,000 meters, with dozens of others close behind. Adding to the magnificence of the ice and snow is the Tasman Glacier, which many skiers find to be the run of a lifetime. New Zealand's highest mountain, Mount Cook, is also found in the park. Named after the English sea captain, James Cook (who never saw it), the mountain reaches skyward to 3,764 meters (12,349 feet) and takes the shape of an almost perfect triangle. Its snow melt runoff creates countless streams that rush down the slopes, merging into rivers. For those who have visited Mount Cook, the mountain remains a vivid memory.

Canterbury has more than its share of New Zealand's natural wonders. Arthur's Pass links Canterbury to the West Coast. When gold was discovered in the West Coast in the early 1860s, colonists flocked to the region. Coming from the east, however, they were blocked by the formidable Southern Alps. A practical, safe passage was needed.

When first found by Arthur Dudley Dobson, who was commissioned by Canterbury authorities to find a "better" way to the west, the pass was difficult and treacherous. However, it was better than the other choices. After digging and building a highway, the pass, named Arthur's Pass, did in fact prove to be practical, if still somewhat dangerous. Today, the pass, which still is an important link between Canterbury and the West Coast, also offers a sightseeing tour of marvelous beauty.

Mackenzie Country, named after the Scotsman James McKenzie but with a minor spelling change, is a highland region bordered by mountains. McKenzie, who was believed to have a sheep dog possessing supernatural powers, allegedly stole thousands of sheep from Canterbury's wealthy wool-kings in the 1850s. He took them to his hidden highlands. Even when finally caught, no prison could hold McKenzie for long and he escaped. In the end, he was pardoned and disappeared. No one heard from him again, though it is said that his ghost, along with that of his faithful dog, still drives sheep in the highlands of Mackenzie Country.

Canterbury is, undoubtedly, one of the most fascinating regions of New Zealand. Its geographical potpourri enables one to experience just about everything New Zealand offers. The region also contains Christchurch, which, with its population of slightly over 300,000, is the largest city of the South Island.

Christchurch

Unlike much of the rest of New Zealand that was colonized without any specific plan, Christchurch, originally a project of the Church of England, was meant to be Anglican in heritage and overseen by English landowners. Although that dream hardly survived beyond the late 1860s, by which time various peoples had settled at Christchurch, its early beginnings have given Christchurch a distinctive air that remains with the city even today.

Early Christchurch was built on the wool trade. The first colonists took vast tracts of flat land suitable for grazing and turned them into the basis for a wealth-producing economic enterprise. Many of these earliest settlers rose to prominence and became what were known as wool-kings. It was observed at the time that Christchurch was in many ways "more English than England." Many residents still find that phrase a compliment.

The city is a pretty one. Designed and built by men with an eye for the practical as well as the beautiful, Christchurch has numerous parks containing flowers and gardens that bloom for most of the year. Architecture, especially buildings constructed in the early days of the city, is reminiscent of England. Indeed some sections of Christchurch can give a visitor the impression that he or she is in England.

The Christchurch of the 1990s is a thoroughly modern city. While the sheep industry is still important, it is far from the only industry. Over 30% of the city's employment is in manufacturing, with many other occupations in service industries.

Christchurch is a bustling city, whose heritage has enabled it to evolve into one of New Zealand's great population centers.

Although some sections may remind one of England, the city has come to embody New Zealand's unique freshness.

Otago

South of Canterbury lies Otago. The coast of this region is quite different than its inland areas. Coastal Otago receives more rainfall, has mild temperatures, and has a greater population; inland areas are dry, there is a wide range of temperature between summer and winter, and the interior has few inhabitants. The western part of the region includes part of the Southern Alps and is dotted by high, deep lakes. Located roughly in the center of the region is an extensive plateau that rises some 600 meters above the sea.

Historic Cardrona Hotel in gold field country, built during the gold rush in Queenstown area of Otago.

Like other areas of New Zealand, gold has a legacy in Otago. Early in the 1860s, the lure of gold swelled the region's population with prospectors and settlers seeking the wealth that gold might bring. The population of Otago soared to some 50,000 within a few years. This was nearly five times more than the early population of the entire region. Towns were built overnight and the gold rush fever made its way to every corner of the region. As on the West Coast, once the gold ran out, most of the mines and many of the towns were abandoned, and only the memories of the gold rush remained.

A second gold rush began with the dredging of Otago's rivers, reaching its zenith in the early 1900s. As with the first gold rush, companies and towns sprang up almost overnight, and at one time nearly 200 dredges were scouring the river beds of the region. Although dredging continued throughout much of this century, the greatest finds came relatively early, and only the most persistent prospectors kept looking for gold.

Today, Otago is best known for its wondrous scenery. During the summer, the interior is hot and dry, almost desertlike; yet in the winter, it is often snow-covered. Some of the mountains are barren, any vegetation having long been washed and scraped away by winds, rain, and snow. The Catlins, on the other hand, is a coastal area that is wild and virtually uninhabited. Its deserted beaches and stark headlands are home to a rare species of penguin (the yellow-eyed penguin), as well as seals. Far inland, to the west, lies Mount Aspiring. The mountain, which is the highlight of the park of the same name, rises more than 3,000 meters above sea level. The park contains lakes, deep valleys, and glaciers. Otago indeed offers a geography that is as distinct as it is memorable.

Much of the land of the region is given to sheep grazing land. Interspersed are orchards, which thrive especially as one nears the coast.

Otago also has its share of industry. The mining of coal and the production of hydroelectric power supply a significant portion of the region's energy needs.

Dunedin

Dunedin is the capital city of Otago. Its 100,000 residents enjoy a city resplendent with Victorian buildings and a serene way of life. Dunedin is an unhurried city, comfortable with its past and confident of its future. In part built on the wealth of the early gold rush, Dunedin provided the capital for many of New Zealand's first businesses. Today, much of the early wealth has spread out throughout the rest of the country, but Dunedin remains a stately city.

The city's setting is both rugged and picturesque. Built on several hills, the city is situated at the end of a long harbor that is volcanic in origin. The harbor is wide and deep enough for ocean-going vessels.

In every respect, Dunedin is a modern, culturally aware city. It offers a variety of industries, has extensive communications and transportation networks, boasts theaters, botanic gardens, and the University of Otago. It also has excellent beaches.

Southland

Milford Sound at Fiordland (Mt. Index on left).

62

The Southland is also called Fiordland. This is the South Island's southernmost extreme. The region is one of contrast. Along the west coast, great fiords cut through mountains that often seem to rise up out of the

Sign at Bluff, on southernmost tip of South Island

sea. The peaks of those mountains are snow-covered, giving the land a semblance of Scandinavia. Fittingly enough, this part of the region is called Fiordland. The terrain here is some of New Zealand's wettest and most desolate. Almost entirely covered with mountains, it is remote, barren, and in many places inaccessible.

To the east, the mountains eventually give way to flatlands interspersed with large lakes. Farther inland stretch vast plains, which support sheep grazing, beef, and agriculture, some of the most important components of the region's prosperity. With less than 4% of New Zealand's population, the Southland accounts for nearly 20% of the country's agricultural exports. This is a rather remarkable statistic, considering that the region has one of the shortest growing seasons in New Zealand. The productivity is a tribute to the hardy and innovative farmers of the Southland, many of whom are descendants of the original Scottish settlers.

Invercargill, with its population of 54,000, is the main city of Southland. Meticulous planning went into the city's building, and today it still has some of the widest streets of any New Zealand city, as well as more park acreage per person than just about anywhere. The city's original wealth was founded on grazing, beef, and farming. While the economy has expanded to include some manufacturing and service occupations, much commercial activity continues to depend on the land.

At one time, some men envisioned Invercargill as becoming a major port city. The New (Oreti) River permitted sailing vessels to reach nearly the heart of the city, but it soon became apparent that Bluff, 27 kilometers (17 miles) to the south, would be a better port. Bluff indeed became the major port of Southland, and remains so today. Ships from around the world dock at Bluff, loading and unloading cargo around the clock. Bluff is also the port that leads across the Foveaux Strait to Stewart Island.

Stewart Island

From Bluff, it takes about 20 minutes by air, or about 2 hours by ferry, to get to Stewart Island. Both the Pacific and Antarctic Oceans touch the island's shores. Stewart Island is the southernmost part of New Zealand, about 65 kilometers (40 miles) long, and 40 kilometers (25 miles) wide.

Rocky outpost on Stewart Island.

The island offers a quiet, though demanding, lifestyle. Most of the 500 or so inhabitants rely on the sea for their livelihood, as did their ancestors. They are a resilient, individual breed who consider themselves unique from the rest of New Zealand. The climate is wet, but the temperatures remain surprisingly mild throughout the year. It is often warmer than much of the Southland. The island is mostly covered with hills and forests. There are only 20 kilometers of roads (about 12 miles), and much of the island remains in its native splendor. Most of the island's native birds and vegetation continue to flourish, free from the interference of civilization.

The island is named after William Stewart, the first officer of the *Pegasus*, a seal-hunting ship. It was one of the first in the waters around the island. The original Maori inhabitants called the island, Rakiura, or "Glowing Sky." There is some debate over why they named it so — after the long days of summer, or because of the auroras that brightened the sky during the winter. Perhaps it was because of both. It is somewhat surprising that the name Stewart remains. Rakiura, Glowing Sky, seems to be a far better description of this southern island.

Although New Zealand's North and South Islands possess distinctive features, they have much in common. Great mountains, snow and glaciers, powerful rivers, deep lakes, rolling plains, rain forests, silver beaches and clean pounding surf — together these make up New Zealand, a land that has a continent full of diversity packed into a relatively small area. Its geographical features have shaped the country, and have molded the people who have settled there. The result is a land that is like nowhere else on our planet.

Chapter Seven
Jobs, Homes, Education

Three of the most important factors in determining what makes a place a good place to live are the area's jobs, homes, and educational opportunities. The quality of these factors combine to make some communities more desirable than others. In New Zealand, without question, there are many fine places to live.

There are exceptionally good jobs throughout the country. There is a particularly strong demand for people with business experience and capital. New Zealand's economy is expanding, stretching throughout the Pacific, and the country offers exciting opportunities for individuals who know how to run a business profitably. Business consultants are sought by many businesses, which in the past were local or regional in scope, but are now setting their sights on the rich markets of Asia.

China, along with the other nations of the Pacific, will be an expanding market throughout the nineties and well into the next century. Many New Zealand businesses have a keen eye on these markets.

New Zealanders are employed in countless occupations. While herding and farming often are the first jobs that come to the minds of people unfamiliar with the nation, there are jobs in engineering, business management, manufacturing, education, government, the service sector — New Zealand offers work similar to the types of work offered in any other advanced nation. With a growing economy, the job base keeps expanding. With the country increasingly focusing on markets throughout the Pacific, it is not surprising that many of the newly created jobs are in businesses which produce goods for export.

While New Zealand offers opportunities in countless occupations, there are many jobs that are as important now as they were in the past. One, sheep herding, helped build the nation.

Sheep Herding

It is estimated that there are some 75 million sheep in New Zealand. Compared to its human population of roughly three million, it is easy to understand the importance of sheep to the country's economy. Without question, the export of meat has been one of New Zealand's economic foundations. Meat, along with wool, continue to be two of the most important of the country's exports.

Sheep herding on South Island.

Although sheep farms are found throughout the country, they are most common in Waikato, Poverty Bay, and Hawkes Bay on the North Island, and in Marlborough, Canterbury, and Southland on the South Island. All these regions have areas of flat land that are excellent for grazing.

Herding is a major industry in the country. Over the years, New Zealanders have developed breeds of sheep for specific areas, matching the characteristics of the animals to the particular climate. Many of the big herders use computers to keep track of their flocks and run their business efficiently. The meat-processing industry is advanced technologically, and is always improving.

Sheep station near Otago, on South Island.

The herding industry is supported by, and in turn supports, many other industries. To keep the pastures fertile for grazing, many New Zealand sheep farmers rely on fertilizers. These are produced in the country, and many types have been developed at the country's agricultural universities. Indeed, New Zealanders are innovators in agricultural technology. As the big farms become more dependent upon technology, many firms scramble to produce the equipment and services they need, from vaccines to keep flocks healthy, to the computers that track the cost of feed as well as the prices in potential markets. Agents are employed to sell the wool and meat throughout the world. Once sold, it requires a modern transportation network to get the wool and meat to markets. A large percentage of New Zealanders rely on the sheep herding industry in one way or another for their own livelihoods.

Sheep herding was a mainstay of New Zealand's economic base in the past, and it is likely to continue to be in the future. The reason is simple: New Zealand wool and meat are in great demand throughout the world.

Homes

Most New Zealanders have the option of living in the city, suburbs, or country. No part of the nation is crowded. There is ample room for New Zealanders as well as newcomers. In fact, New Zealand has one of the lowest population densities of any developed country.

Original settlers' house on South Island.

Whether a person chooses to live in the city or not, he has the opportunity to buy land with his home. Most New Zealanders own a three- or four-bedroom house set on a good-sized parcel of property, usually about one-fifth of an acre. Although the size of property varies, depending on where one is living, the fifth of an acre is the average lot size. Because most of New Zealand's cities have been built along practical lines, and tend to sprawl outward from their central hubs, even city dwellers are not denied owning comfortable lots.

Most buildings are constructed of either brick, wood, weatherboard, or stucco. Since wood used in building is treated with preservatives, there is little deterioration and New Zealanders seldom hesitate to use it in their houses if it achieves the look they wish to attain. Most of the new homes are designed to require as little maintenance as possible. In other words, they are built to last.

Buying a Home in New Zealand

When considering buying a home in New Zealand, whether one is a citizen or immigrant, the following guidelines will prove helpful:

♦ Before committing himself to any kind of transaction, the home buyer should be familiar with the area he desires. The immigrant, in particular, should become familiar with the various regions of the country, the local and national economy, and decide which area will best meet his lifestyle needs.

♦ To help in seeking and buying a home, the potential buyer should obtain the services of a reputable real estate agent. Potential buyers should always avoid dealing with individuals who promise that they can help the person buy "the house of your dreams with significant savings." Reputable real estate agents are members of the New Zealand Real Estate Institute. Working with them ensures that any transactions will be done properly, according to the law. Moreover, many real estate agents are experienced in working with immigrants; they are aware of the immigrant's needs and can guide him through legal channels.

• Potential buyers should be willing to ask questions to clarify any matter or confusion that may arise. New Zealand real estate agents have earned the reputation of being quite helpful. Furthermore, virtually all offer complete services to make home buying easy and enjoyable.

Because of New Zealand's growth over the last several years, and, just as importantly, its promise of continued growth in the future, the real estate market has prospered. When people buy homes in New Zealand, they are making a smart and worthwhile investment.

Education

Education in New Zealand is world-class. Indeed, many of New Zealand's teachers are innovators, and their ideas are embraced in other countries. The United States, for example, has looked to New Zealand as a source of ideas and practical applications in the fields of cooperative education and the whole-language approach to teaching, reading and writing.

New Zealand is a literate country. Free public education is guaranteed to all citizens, and the people look upon education as an important right. Communities support the education system, and hold learning in high esteem.

It is New Zealanders' regard for knowledge that leads them to constantly question the system, and strive to improve it. This comes even as other countries look to New Zealand for leadership in education. So valued is New Zealand's education system by others that many foreign students enroll each year in the nation's universities.

One American educator familiar with education in New Zealand recently remarked: "There are wonderful ideas and programs coming to the United States out of New Zealand schools." There are even more exceptional programs in New Zealand.

Education Starts When Children Are Young

Close to 50% of the country's three-year-olds, and up to 90% of the four-year-olds, receive some type of preschooling. Many children start formal school when they are five, though compulsory education begins at six.

The country is quite accommodating to immigrants. Even children whose first language is not English are accepted into mainstream education. The Kiwi Melting Pot is as apparent in the area of education as it is throughout the rest of the country.

The type of school children attend is dependent upon where they live. In some areas, a student's primary education might be completed at a full primary school, an intermediate school, or a one-to-seven school. Primary schools are required to be open for a minimum of 400 half-days a year.

Supplementing the public education system are a number of private schools that are found throughout the country. School attendance is compulsory through the age of 15; however, over 90% of New Zealand's students remain in school and graduate. Many go on to college.

The typical school curriculum is similar to the studies undertaken in the traditional American or European school. Subjects such as English, reading, spelling, mathematics, social studies, science, and health are required. Other subjects include physical education, art, and music. Some state primary schools are bilingual, and Maori is taught in yet others.

The school year is divided into three terms. Although the individual dates vary among the schools, in general, schools are in session much of the year, with a short vacation in May and a longer one in December and January, which coincides with the New Zealand summer.

As students continue through secondary school, their studies become more specialized. Secondary schools are required to remain open a minimum of 380 half-days each year. Passing the School Certificate examination is necessary for students to pass into the next secondary level. The School Certificate is much like the high-school diploma in the United States, and is considered to be essential for employment. The Sixth Form Certificate is the next degree, followed by a Higher School Certificate. Both of these are awarded after rigorous examinations. Exacting standards help to ensure the quality of New Zealand schools throughout the educational system.

The Universities — Repositories of Knowledge

New Zealand has several major universities: Victoria University (in Wellington), Canterbury University, The University of Otago, Massey University (in Palmerston), and Waikato University. While each offers a variety of courses in many curriculums, they also specialize in particular areas, as the following breakdown shows:

Victoria University — public administration, architecture, and social services.
Canterbury University — engineering and forestry. Also has an excellent fine arts program.
The University of Otago — medicine, pharmacy, dentistry, mineral technology, and surveying.
Massey University — agriculture, veterinary science, and food technology.
Waikato University — law, management, and teaching.

Of course, even though they may not specialize in a specific field, other colleges offer degree courses in numerous subject areas. Moreover, the quality of the education at all is of the highest standard.

Students who wish to continue with an advanced education are not limited to attending only universities. Students intending to become teachers are most likely to enroll in one of the many colleges of education. New Zealand also has many community colleges, business schools, and technical institutes. In addition, many communities support adult evening schools for those who wish to pursue their education after working hours. There are also correspondence courses available for people who wish to fit their education into busy schedules.

New Zealanders understand that education is the key to the future. They elevate learning to a national priority.

The Foundation of the Country

Together, jobs, homes, and education form the foundation on which modern New Zealand is built. If one were to ask a person what makes life pleasurable, it is likely that the answer would include having a nice place to live and working at a job that is satisfying and fulfilling. Upon further reflection, it would become clear that a well-rounded education is a crucial requirement for both.

New Zealand offers all three prerequisites for pleasure. While much of the rest of the world struggles with high unemployment, falling living standards, substandard housing, and troubled schools, New Zealand clearly emerges as a country to be envied.

Chapter Eight
Communication and Transportation

If anything denotes a technologically advanced country of the nineties, posed for dramatic growth into the next century, it is the communication and transportation systems of the nation. Unquestionably, we are in the information age. Intricately interwoven with the transfer of information is communication. Quite simply, information cannot be exchanged and shared rapidly without modern communications.

A quality transportation system is just as important. People and products depend on efficient roads, rail links, and airways if they are to move quickly and easily. In many respects, the modern world is built on the flow of information, people, and products.

Modern Communications

As the advanced world moves into the information age, New Zealand is at the forefront. There are several reasons for this. Despite its many mountains, New Zealand is a small country. It has a strong economy and an educated populace. Moreover, as business grows, its reliance on technology grows, expanding the need for modern communications. Since the country is relatively small in area, it is a simple matter to ensure that the country's communication network is among the best in the world.

A Communications Giant

One of the major communications providers of the country is Telecom Corporation of New Zealand, Ltd. Telecom is an international corporation, part owned by Bell Atlantic and Ameritech, two American telecommunications giants, and Fay Richwhite and Freightways, two New Zealand companies. Employing over 11,000 people and with assets of close to $5 billion, Telecom owns one of the most technologically advanced communications networks in the world.

Over 95% of Telecom's lines are connected to digital exchanges. This is significant for businesses to be competitive on a world-scale, because digital exchanges can carry more information than older lines. Digital lines also easily handle the newest technologies in communications such as data and video transmissions. For example, through Telecom, businesses can conduct video conferences efficiently and effectively.

Telecom is not concerned with only business customers. The service it provides the New Zealand public is both efficient and reasonably priced. Phone booths, known as call boxes, are located throughout the country, making it easy for New Zealanders to stay in touch with each other.

Telecom's service and the quality of its products are enviable. Phone service is reliable with leading-edge computers handling the routing of calls. The company not only maintains communications lines, it distributes many of the telecommunications products in New Zealand, from telephones to sophisticated computer linkups and networks. It also offers a cellular network that covers close to 100% of the country's populated areas; it provides mobile radio service; and it provides services for pagers. Telecom's success is a model for communications companies the world over.

Competition Spurs Innovation

One of the reasons Telecom presses ahead to remain at the forefront of communications innovation is Clear Communications, Ltd. Begun in 1990, Clear was started as an option for customers who felt Telecom was not fully meeting their needs. Like Telecom, Clear is backed by several major corporations and is international in scope. Todd Corporation, Television New Zealand, Bell Canada, and MCI (the U.S. communications giant) all have holdings in Clear. Their backing ensures Clear of capital and technical expertise.

Clear provides a variety of services to both business and residential customers. The company has grown fast. By 1993, it had already cornered over 15% of the New Zealand toll market. Clear can connect its customers to any fixed phone in New Zealand, as well as internationally.

Realizing the importance of compatible technology, Clear customers can use their existing equipment to take advantage of Clear's lines. Clear focuses its service on providing switching facilities and digital transmission; its lines include fiber-optic cable, which has begun only recently to be installed in the communications networks of many other advanced nations.

Keeping Up with the News

Perhaps because New Zealand is an island, which, since the time of its colonization by Europeans, had to look outward to keep abreast of world events, New Zealanders still tend to look out to the world for news. The country enjoys a variety of news organs, including newspapers, magazines, TV and radio, as well as on-line computer services. New Zealand may be somewhat isolated because of the Pacific, but it is far from isolated in terms of information, thanks to our electronic age.

New Zealanders are serious when they try to keep up with the news. The evidence is plain: New Zealanders, when their population is compared with the populations of other countries, buy more newspapers than people just about anywhere else. Many cities are serviced by several newspapers. While all the large cities have at least one newspaper, and often more than one, even the small cities have daily papers. Many New Zealand households receive the paper in the morning and read it during breakfast. The typical newspaper carries both world and local news.

Certainly newspapers are not the only method for getting the news. New Zealanders also have access to numerous magazines. Major news magazines such as *Time* and *Newsweek* can be found each week at bookstores and news agents (similar to newspaper stands in the U.S.). General-interest magazines that are written for various target audiences are published regularly and have consistent readerships. A variety of trade magazines are available as well.

New Zealanders also have the option of gaining information through television and radio. Unlike the United States and many of the countries of Europe, where television became a fixture in many homes during the 1950s and 1960s, TV came to New Zealand later. Now, however, the country has stations broadcasting on both the VHF and UHF spectrums. With satellite broadcasting, even more stations will be available.

There are numerous radio stations throughout the country. Most of the major population centers have several stations that broadcast everything from music to news to discussion shows. In fact, there are few areas which do not enjoy good radio reception.

Because of their fine school system, New Zealanders are literate and informed. They continue to have a yearning for information and knowledge as adults. Of course, by staying informed of world and local events, New Zealanders arm themselves with the knowledge they need to make the decisions necessary for success in today's world.

Modern Transportation

New Zealanders enjoy a wide variety of transportation options. The country is crisscrossed by a superior system of roads, has excellent air service, and adequate rail lines. Water travel is yet another method of transportation.

On the whole, New Zealanders enjoy traveling, not only in their own country, but in other lands as well. Indeed, many New Zealanders visit other countries.

Cars — for Most, the First Choice

Many of New Zealand's roads are paved, well-maintained, and sufficiently sign-posted so that travelers can motor easily from one place to another. Many of the roadways offer panoramic views of incredible countryside. Driving is on the left-hand side of the road, and most roads accommodate all kinds of vehicles.

Car travel is preferred by many New Zealanders, who enjoy being able to drive to the parks, beaches, and other entertainment sites that are found throughout the nation. Most New Zealand families own one car, and many own two. Gasoline is relatively inexpensive by world standards. Condensed natural gas is fast becoming an alternative fuel for motor vehicles, and many vehicles have been outfitted to use this energy source. It is worthy to note that natural gas as a motor-vehicle fuel is just starting to be utilized in the United States. It appears that New Zealanders are one of the first nations to recognize this important alternative fuel.

For people who prefer not to drive themselves, modern bus and train services operate throughout the country. Chauffeur-driven cars are also available, and major cities have round-the-clock taxi service.

Rail Service

Trains operate throughout the country, but because much of New Zealand is mountainous and hilly, train tracks are of narrow gauge. This limits the comfort of trains, as well as the type of cargo that can be shipped. Still, comfortable passenger service links many of the major cities, especially Auckland and Wellington on the North

Island, and Christchurch and Invercargill on the South Island. Of course, the scenery along rail lines is outstanding.

There are several rail services that cater primarily to tourists. Between Christchurch and Greymouth on the South Island, for example, is *The Tranzalpine*, a train that travels through the Southern Alps. In 1988, this train won a New Zealand Tourism Award.

Historic steam train on South Island.

Air Service

New Zealand is well serviced by several airlines. Virtually all of the major cities enjoy air service, with smaller airlines maintaining routes from the cities to resort areas. Smaller airlines also service many of the smaller towns and less populated regions. Virtually all fly modern aircraft.

The four main airline centers are Auckland, Wellington, Christchurch, and Dunedin. However, even remote areas of the country can be reached by air, and then a short trip by car. Some airlines provide tours, and are able, for example, to take off and land on water, or land on skis atop glaciers.

Air New Zealand is the nation's own international carrier. Its standards are high, and it enjoys a worldwide reputation for excellence. Air New Zealand provides a modern fleet that flies from Auckland, Wellington, and Christchurch to locations in Australia, the U.S., Europe, and Asia.

Air New Zealand is not the only major airline servicing the country. Other airlines maintain routes into and out of New Zealand. Just a few include: United Airlines, Continental, Qantas, Japan Air Lines, and British Airways. Many cities, including Hong Kong and Singapore, also maintain air links with New Zealand.

Travel by Water

Surrounded by water, separated by water, and covered with rivers and lakes, New Zealanders have developed a close affinity with water. Connecting the North and South Islands is the Interislander ferry service, which carries passengers from Wellington across the Cook Strait and through the Marlborough Sound to Picton. The trip takes about three hours. Although Cook Strait is known for its high winds, once the ferry enters Marlborough Sound, the traveler is greeted by beautiful bays, inlets, and mountains that plunge directly into the sea.

Water is not only used for travel, but for pleasure. New Zealanders are boaters. Many families, especially those who live near a waterway, own a boat and use it often. On a fair day, many bays near major cities are filled with boat traffic.

The sea also provides a means for shipping goods. Most coastal cities are port cities, acting as way stations for products that flow into New Zealand from other countries, and also as shipping points that enable New Zealand exports to make their way to foreign ports. For New Zealanders, the sea provides an economical means of shipping goods around the world.

Overseas Travel

New Zealanders have a reputation for being world travelers. Some of the more popular destinations include Australia, the various islands of the Pacific, the United States, and Europe. Asia is increasingly becoming a destination for traveling New Zealanders.

This worldly travel has helped New Zealanders become accustomed to what the rest of the world offers, and compare it to their own homes. Few New Zealanders find their own country lacking.

By any measure, New Zealand's communications and transportation systems and networks are among the best in the world. While the communications industry forges ahead with cutting-edge technology, the country's superior roadways, air links, and shipping routes ensure that people and goods can be transported within the country and internationally quickly and efficiently.

Possessing an efficient system of disseminating information in conjunction with a modern infrastructure helps to position New Zealand for dramatic growth in the future. The country truly is a land of opportunity.

Chapter Nine
New Zealand's Economy

In the past, New Zealand's economy was largely dependent on the export of wool, meat, and dairy products. Consequently, any downturn in world prices and demand would severely affect the economy. All that has changed during the last few decades.

As New Zealand has pursued global trading partners, and while wool, meat, and dairy products continue to be important to the country's economy, New Zealand has become a major player in world trade. Along with its traditional products, the nation exports significant amounts of fish, produce, forestry products, and manufactured goods. In addition, New Zealand exports fine jewelry to Europe and heavy machinery to Asian nations.

Tourism is yet another major segment of New Zealand's economy. The country is the destination for visitors from around the world, and its popularity as a vacation spot is growing rapidly.

Each of these areas is of enough importance to examine them in greater detail. First, we will look at agriculture, which remains a mainstay on the country's economic balance sheets.

Agriculture

New Zealand exports close to 90% of its agricultural products. Indeed, agriculture accounts for almost 60% of New Zealand's export earnings. When one considers the many other businesses that support and contribute to the country's agricultural industry, it is easy to understand the importance that farming and grazing have for New Zealanders. A large part of the workforce depends on agriculture either directly or in a supporting role. Much of New Zealand's land is ideal for dairy farming and for raising cattle and sheep. In most areas, the weather is mild, making it unnecessary to house livestock during winters, and grass grows throughout much of the year. Although estimates vary, the livestock population has been calculated at nearly 75 million sheep, some eight million head of cattle, and more than a half-million pigs.

New Zealanders don't just raise livestock, however. Grain-growing includes such staples as wheat, barley, and oats. Corn is also a major crop, as are potatoes, peas, apples, pears, and tobacco. Kiwifruit and pipfruit are fast becoming major crops as well. Because the country uses modern, high-tech farming equipment and methods, productivity is among the highest in the world.

Most farms are family-owned and -operated. Since farming is an export business in New Zealand, farmers strive for the efficiency that is necessary to compete in world markets. They are quite successful, as the following figures show.

+ Meat and wool exports totaled over $3 billion a year.
+ Exports of dairy products totaled over $2 billion a year.
+ Exports of grains and fruits totaled over $1 billion a year.

Keep in mind that these farming achievements have come from a country that has a population of less than 3.5 million people.

Here are some equally impressive facts:

+ New Zealand usually exports over 270,000 tons of wool each year. This is close to 70% of the wool traded in international markets.
+ 50% of the mutton traded throughout the world comes from New Zealand.
+ New Zealand agricultural exports regularly total more than 50% of the country's total exports.

Agriculture is an area that draws strong interest from both New Zealand and international investors. A company that is one of the leaders in agricultural investments is Wrightson. The company, which is a subsidiary of Fletcher Challenge Ltd., one of New Zealand's largest companies, is a world-scale concern in agriculture. Wrightson boasts assets of over $400 million and operates branches in every New Zealand city and major town. A large, dedicated workforce provides support and advice on virtually everything that has to do with agriculture.

Wrightson's experience extends to far more than just farming, however. It is also one of New Zealand's foremost companies in real estate, wool, livestock, grains, and seed. It has significant operations in agricultural finance, as well as agricultural commodities. The company provides expertise in farm investment, helping investors not only to acquire holdings, but helping them manage those holdings so that they achieve profits.

Despite its size, New Zealand is one of the world's leading exporters of dairy products and wool. That is quite a tribute to a country of its size and population.

Manufacturing

During the past thirty years, manufacturing has made steady gains as an important sector of New Zealand's overall economy. At one time, manufacturing centered on the production and processing of dairy and meat products.

Today, the country's manufacturing base is far more diversified. The production of machinery, paper and paper products, lumber, clothing, motor vehicles, refined petroleum, and printed materials are important industries. Auckland is the principal manufacturing region, although many other cities are emerging as smaller, specialized centers.

Since the early 1970s, the mineral output of the country has increased substantially. This in turn has helped support the expansion of the manufacturing base. Several important minerals are produced, including: gold, silver, limestone, iron ore, silica sand, and pumice.

Energy

New deposits of oil and natural gas have been discovered in various regions, and their development has added to the country's overall energy output. However, New Zealand is not widely known for its production of fossil fuels; rather, it is known for its production of hydroelectric power.

Close to 75% of New Zealand's electricity is produced by hydroelectric plants, which is not surprising given the country's abundance of powerful rivers. Much of the remaining electricity is produced by plants that burn coal or oil. Still, the use of so many hydroelectric facilities helps to keep the threat of air pollution to a minimum, which is always a major consideration to New Zealanders.

Large hydroelectric plants are on the Waikato River on the North Island, and on the Waitaki River on the South Island. In addition to hydroelectric power, underground steam is used to produce significant amounts of electricity on the North Island. Geothermal energy, which makes this type of electrical production possible, is used in other places around the world and is becoming an important alternative energy source. New Zealand is one of the leaders in this developing technology.

Although New Zealand imports some petroleum and petroleum products, the country is far from being dependent upon foreign exporters of oil. Unlike some other countries around the world whose industrial lifeblood depends on oil imports, New Zealand is insulated from the fluctuation of world oil markets because of its own energy production. This helps to ensure a relatively stable economy.

Fishing and Forestry

Surrounded by ocean and with many regions covered by forests, it is easy to see why fishing and forestry would be major areas of New Zealand's economy. In some parts of the country, these are the dominant economic enterprises. Both freshwater and saltwater fish are popular in New Zealand, for domestic consumption and export. The species most in demand include: crayfish, oysters, snapper, flounder, and sole. Crayfish and oysters often account for nearly half of the total annual tonnage.

Timber production is another important industry. Although several forests fell victim to early colonization, an extensive reforestation plan over the years has restored trees to many areas. Lumber companies today actively manage their forests, ensuring that new stocks of trees replace those used in the production of building materials, newsprint, and paper board.

Foreign Trade

New Zealand is a major player in the global marketplace. Its most frequent trading partners are Australia, Great Britain, the United States, Europe, and the nations of the Pacific.

New Zealand is one of the world's important trading nations. It is a world leader in the export of agricultural products, and is a significant exporter of machinery and various manufactured goods. New Zealand wool is prized around the world.

While New Zealand exports much of what it produces, it imports the materials it needs. Major imports include some types of manufactured products and heavy machinery, oil, chemicals, iron, steel, and textiles. Many of its imports come from Australia, Great Britain, the United States, Japan, and Singapore.

Several companies have proven very successful in foreign trade, particularly in exporting. Consider these significant facts:

- The Fortex Group Ltd. has a major contract to supply venison to Europe. Begun in 1971 as a company that focused its business on beef, Fortex eventually expanded to include deer farming. The company does close to $250 million worth of business in exporting.
- Advanced Door Systems Ltd. of Christchurch designs and builds garage door openers. Started in 1987, the company is known for its quality, design and efficiency.
- In 1985, two brothers founded Cedenco Foods Ltd. Originally, Cedenco's business focused on producing tomato paste for export. The company has since expanded to process various fruits and pumpkins. Cedenco derives much of its profits from the 17 companies to which it sends its products.
- T.L. Jones Ltd. manufactures and markets a protection system for elevator doors. The company exports close to 80% of its products to Australia, North America, Europe, and several countries in Asia.

These companies are just a few examples of the many that have helped make New Zealand an important exporting nation. Their ingenuity and innovation have resulted in the production of goods that are in demand throughout the world. As the reputation for quality and design of New Zealand products grows, that demand will only rise, promising a bright future for the New Zealand economy.

While New Zealand trades with many countries around the world, it has always enjoyed a special relationship with Australia. The two countries have long enjoyed both cultural and economic links. In 1983, the two countries agreed to CER, the Australia-New Zealand Closer Economic Relation Trade Agreement. The original agreement sought to establish free trade between the two countries by 1995, but free trade was achieved much sooner, in 1990.

Unlike some trade agreements, CER does not create a trading bloc whereby New Zealand and Australia — while establishing free trade with each other — erect barriers to trade and duties against the products of other countries. Because the agreement promotes free trade without putting into place burdensome restrictions aimed at the rest of the world, New Zealand enjoys greater access to Australian markets while still having easy access to trade with other countries. Furthermore, because of CER, New Zealand has better access to Australia's larger market. This is an important advantage to New Zealand, which has a relatively small population in comparison to Australia.

In addition to trade issues, CER addresses various other factors that affect trade. For example, the agreement includes provisions for aid to industry, the unification of laws pertaining to business, customs procedures, and the solving of problems that might adversely affect trade.

Without question, despite its having a small population and being somewhat isolated from the rest of the world, New Zealand has developed a significant trading economy. While most of the country's companies remain relatively small, it does have several large, multinational corporations that are truly worldwide in their enterprises.

Tourism

Tourism is a major industry in New Zealand and an important part of the country's overall economy. During the past decade, tourism has increased an average of 8% per year, which is roughly double the percentage at which tourism has increased throughout the rest of the world. In 1992, more than one million people visited New Zealand, and by the turn of the century that number is expected to surpass the three-million-per-year mark. Already, tourism accounts for close to $3 billion in foreign exchange, which is more than either meat or wool.

While tourists come from the world over, Australians, Americans, Germans, and Japanese seem to predominate. Many visitors also come from Great Britain, Canada, Singapore, Hong Kong, and Taiwan.

90

Despite its growth in recent years, many experts feel that New Zealand's tourism industry is positioned for even greater growth in the coming years. Perhaps most importantly, tourists are drawn to New Zealand's spectacular natural beauty. Few places offer mountains and oceans, swimming and skiing in such close proximity in such an agreeable climate.

On the whole, New Zealand has not yet begun to take full advantage of tourism. Many places in the country have not utilized their attractions and promoted them to the tourists. This does not mean that New Zealanders do not welcome tourists; rather, many areas have not marketed themselves for the tourist industry. There is much potential growth for tourism throughout the country.

Indeed, tourism is one of New Zealand's major growth industries. There is plenty of room for innovative, imaginative people who can plan for the needs of visitors and provide the services they require.

One of the unique aspects of New Zealand tourists is the fact that many visitors return to the country after their initial visit, and many of these people choose to stay. One of the best investment opportunities in the country is tourism. Those individuals with expertise in the tourism industry are frequently impressed with the opportunity to start a business in a country that is only beginning to realize its potential in relation to the rest of the world.

The government recognizes the value of tourism in attracting foreign investment. Consequently, the government supports the tourist industry, because it understands that key investment in New Zealand can come from overseas. The New Zealand Tourism Board has been established to coordinate private and public initiatives in tourism.

Whereas many of the advanced countries around the world struggle with serious economic problems that in the long run affect the living standards of their citizens, New Zealand is poised for solid economic growth. Once, the country relied on wool, meat, and dairy products as the foundation of its economy. Today, while those industries are still important, manufacturing, energy production, various agricultural enterprises, a strong, vital exporting sector, and tourism, which is a result of the country's many natural wonders, clean air, and friendly people, all combine to ensure New Zealand's economic future.

Chapter Ten
Business Opportunities and Investment in New Zealand

The investment opportunities in New Zealand are excellent. The government encourages both domestic and foreign investment. Restrictions are few and regulations are practical, designed so that the government can monitor investments on the national level as well as in specific areas.

Foreign investment, in fact, is vital to the continued growth of New Zealand's economy. While most foreign investment in the past has come from Great Britain, Australians have become major investors, with investors from the United States and Japan also being important.

New Zealand offers several advantages to potential investors, including:

- Easy access to the markets of Australia, particularly true since the signing of CER, the Australia-New Zealand Closer Economic Relation Trade Agreement.
- Low inflation.
- A very stable political climate.
- A skilled labor force.
- Competitive labor costs.
- A modern standard of living.
- An economy that is linked to nations around the world.

Certain investments require approval through particular ministries or agencies. For example, the Overseas Investment Commission (OIC) grants government approval for foreign investment in rural land, deep-water fishing, and broadcasting. In addition, an overseas investor or company that desires to buy some types of land must obtain authorization from the Land Valuation Tribunal. These lands include farmland, offshore islands, reserves, or land noted as having historical or archeological significance. Investment in enterprises concerned with natural resources also requires specific licenses and consents, either from the Minister of Energy or the Minister of Conservation. Major mergers or takeovers, especially when such ventures may affect competition, must obtain the consent of the Commerce Commission.

Although restrictions, in some cases as noted above, apply for certain types of investments, there are many agencies designed to assist investors. Some of the most important include:

- The Ministry of External Relations and Trade (MERT). MERT promotes relations with possible exporting nations through various trade missions.
- The Export Guarantee Office (ExGO). This agency offers various services, including information on international markets, market advice, banking and credit insurance.
- The New Zealand Export/Import Corporation. The purpose of this group is to increase the export opportunities for New Zealand companies.
- The Regional Development Investigation Grant Scheme. Grants are made available to cover some of the costs involved in studying what the possible results might be when new activities are introduced to a region. The maximum grant is $50,000 and is available for up to 50% of the costs of the study.
- The Department of Labor. This department provides subsidies for programs that create jobs. It also offers advice on employment and training subsidies.

All of these organizations and units clearly show that New Zealand is serious about investment. While maintaining the necessary controls, the government has also taken the initiative to welcome investment and assist investors in any way it can.

Business Organizations

New Zealand businesses may be organized in any one of several ways. Business may be conducted by individuals, partners and joint ventures, companies, or trusts.

Individuals, also called *sole proprietors,* need not register with any agency to conduct business. Many New Zealand businesses are run by individuals. Although there are few restrictions on sole proprietorships, the sole proprietor is fully responsible for all the obligations and debts of the business. On the other hand, the sole proprietor enjoys all the profits.

Partnerships and *joint ventures* may be entered into and operated by two or more individuals, groups of individuals, trusts, companies, or any combination of these. The purpose of any partnership or joint venture is for the participants to work together so that profits can be realized. In most of these business arrangements, formal agreements or contracts are signed which clearly state the responsibilities and rights of each partner. Such agreements cover all aspects of the business, with particular focus on the sharing of profits and losses.

In addition, the following specifics need to be noted regarding partnerships:

♦ Since partners are responsible for any debts and obligations of the partnership, partners may be sued for debts owed by the partnership.
♦ In special partnerships, or joint ventures, partners who are categorized only as investors may be shielded from some liabilities. Of course, in such cases, these partners usually do not

equally share the profits. Any contracts or agreements must clearly detail special relationships like this.

♦ Salaries paid to relatives who are employed in a partnership must be reasonable. Salaries for employees should coincide with the typical wage for the work being done.

♦ In trading partnerships, all partners must sign a written agreement with the working partner that clearly details all duties that are required as well as the salary to be paid. This is essential if the salary is to be deductible from the income of the business. Such payments are considered salary or wages and are taxed accordingly.

♦ In businesses owned by a husband and wife, it is not necessary to operate as a formal partnership; however, it is generally advisable to organize in this manner.

Trusts may be created either by will or by deed. If the design of the trust directs them to, the trustees may conduct business in the name and interests of the trust. There are several trustee companies that offer a variety of trust services in New Zealand.

Companies, better known as *limited liability companies*, are the most common means of conducting business in the country. The most important legislation directed to companies is the Companies Act of 1955, which was significantly amended in 1994. Based on similar British law, the Act, including subsequent amendments, addresses the steps necessary for the starting and operation of companies in New Zealand. To fill in any gaps left by the Companies Act, additional legislation has been passed for specialized co-operative companies in primary industries.

Two other acts, the Securities Act of 1978 and the Securities Regulations of 1983, regulate the offering of securities to the public. This includes the offering of company shares and prospectuses.

In recent years, there have been some changes to the Companies Act, including:

+ In some circumstances, notably when officers of the company do not maintain proper records regarding accounts, or conduct business in a reckless or fraudulent manner, said officers may be held personally liable for any debts and liabilities of the company that are a result of the officers' actions.
+ Related companies may be required to contribute to the payment of debts of each other.
+ Companies are now considered to have the rights, powers, and privileges of an individual.
+ Procedures for changing a company's objectives are less demanding. A company may be registered without providing a statement of its objectives.

A new Companies Bill, which was designed to modernize New Zealand's laws regulating business, was approved in 1994. The bill was based primarily on similar laws in North America and updated New Zealand's earlier Companies Act. The new bill contained many provisions, but these are some of the most important:

+ The distinction between private and public companies was abolished. All companies exist under the same rules.
+ Companies are permitted to buy back their own shares; and are allowed to offer financial assistance toward the purchase of their own shares.
+ The concepts of par value and nominal capital were abolished.
+ A company may have as few as one shareholder and director.
+ The bill includes protections of minority rights.
+ The duties of directors of a company are expressly detailed.
+ Rules for liquidation have been simplified.
+ The distributions of the company are to be subject to the director's satisfaction that the company is solvent.
+ Transactions that involve more than 50% of the assets of a company require the approval of the shareholders.
+ Companies that are based overseas are required to file annual accounts if they conduct business in New Zealand.

These changes are not burdensome to business. Indeed, they are designed to bring New Zealand's business law up to date with the laws of other advanced nations.

Incorporation

Companies that desire to incorporate and carry out business in New Zealand must obtain registration, which is granted by the Registrar of Companies. To obtain registration, a company must comply with some important regulations.

First, the company must file the Memorandum of Association. The memorandum includes the factors under which the company is incorporated. At its basic, the memorandum includes the company's name, the share of capital, and the current shareholders. It is not necessary to state the company's objective, but many provide that simply as a matter of course.

The company must also file the Articles of Association, which detail the procedures and purposes of management. Other basic data, such as information about the directors and secretary, address of registered office, and the securing of the approval of the Registrar of Companies for the company's name, must be attended to.

In actuality, the process is neither long, nor complicated. For most companies, the name approval is obtained within a week or two. At the time of application to the Registrar of Companies, a name may be reserved for the applicant. The company then has three months to register, after which the reservation lapses. In actuality, there are no particular restrictions on companies, including foreign companies, who are, in fact, encouraged to do business in New Zealand. However, it should be noted that overseas companies cannot establish a place of business in the country unless their name is reserved.

Reporting Requirements and General Meetings

After incorporation, there are few reporting requirements. New Zealand companies are not overburdened with regulatory paperwork.

New Zealand companies that are incorporated and that have capital must file annual returns which include the following:

1. The address of the registered office.
2. The names of the directors and secretary.
3. The total amount of debt.
4. Share capital.
5. Past and present members dated back to the last list.

In addition to the required reporting, publicly owned companies must hold an annual general meeting of the shareholders. Private companies are not required to have an annual general meeting, provided that the concerns and resolutions that are typically conducted at the annual meeting are done at other times.

The Types of Companies

Companies in New Zealand may be of three main types:

♦ Unlimited Companies, in which there is no limit to the liability of owners.
♦ Companies Limited by Guarantee, in which the liabilities of the owners are limited by a predetermined amount.
♦ Companies Limited by Shares, in which the liability of owners is limited to the amount unpaid on their shares in the company.

Most companies in New Zealand fall under that third category. Companies Limited by Shares may in turn take one of three forms: Public Companies, Private Companies, and Overseas Companies. We will now examine each.

Public Companies

A public company must have at least seven members, two directors and a secretary. It may offer shares to the public, provided it conforms to the rules contained in the Securities Act of 1978 and the Securities Regulations of 1983.

Should the company wish to apply for listing on the New Zealand Stock Exchange, it must satisfy specific requirements regarding accounts and shareholders. A company can obtain detailed information explaining the requirements from the Stock Exchange.

Public companies must hold an annual general meeting in which they present the company's business activities of the year to the shareholders. During the annual meeting, audited accounts are also presented to the shareholders, after which the accounts must be given to the Registrar of Companies and made available to the public for inspection.

The company's accounts must be audited by a Chartered Accountant. The audit must disclose information about the company's operation as detailed by the Companies Act. Before the audit can be presented to shareholders, it must be signed by two directors.

Private Companies

Private companies must have at least two members, a director and a secretary, but memberships are usually limited to 25 people. A private company may not offer shares to the public. A private company's accounts need not be audited, provided the members all agree. The accounts do not have to be lodged with the Registrar of Companies.

Overseas Companies

An overseas company is defined as a company which has been formed or incorporated in a country other than New Zealand.

Before they can establish a place of business, overseas companies must receive approval for their name.

Within 30 days of the establishment of business, the company must file the following with the Registrar of Companies:

+ Evidence of incorporation.
+ A certified copy of the company's charter or constitution.
+ A list of its directors and secretary.
+ The name of a resident of New Zealand who will act as the company's agent.

Similar to public companies, overseas companies must have their accounts audited by a Chartered Accountant annually. The record of the accounts must then be presented to the Registrar of Companies, along with information of the company's overall business activity throughout the world.

All companies that are registered with the Registrar of Companies must file an annual return that includes information regarding directors, secretary, registered office, secured liabilities, and shareholdings. For those companies that do not file audited accounts, a certified copy of the unanimous resolution of the members agreeing not to file must be presented instead.

While the government provides laws and regulations that companies in New Zealand must follow, the general business climate in New Zealand is geared for growth. Various agencies exist to support both domestic and overseas companies. Unquestionably, this positive atmosphere for business has enabled New Zealand to position itself as an important trading nation in the world market.

Chapter Eleven
Investment Opportunities

While New Zealand, on the whole, has enjoyed excellent economic growth throughout this century, the country is on the verge of an even better future. Unlike some advanced nations that look upon business — and particularly business taxes — as a way to alleviate the staggering problems that they face, New Zealanders look upon business as a means of making life better for everyone through enhanced economic opportunity. The government promotes a positive business climate, while at the same time providing the proper regulations to ensure that economic growth does not come at unacceptable social or environmental costs. New Zealanders work hard to keep their environment, society, and economy in harmony.

To encourage business, the government provides a variety of incentives available through several agencies such as the New Zealand Export/Import Corporation, the Export Guarantee Office (ExGO), the Ministry of External Relations and Trade (MERT), the Regional Development Investigation Grant Scheme, and the Department of Labor. These were discussed in detail in Chapter 10.

In addition, in the government's continuing efforts to reduce official intervention in the affairs of business, and to assist business whenever possible, several other agencies have been formed. These include:

- The New Zealand Trade Development Board (TDB). The purpose of the board is to promote export trade. Its consultants offer various services to exporters.
- The Investment Unit of the Ministry of Commerce. This unit offers advice to investors who wish to set up a business in New Zealand. It also provides support in the way of immigration of individuals who are setting up a business in the country.

The result of this support for business has been a surge in economic opportunity in several regions. Both the North and South Islands offer many prime investment opportunities.

New Zealand's Investment Advantages

Along with the incentives available throughout its economic framework, New Zealand offers potential investors several other advantages. While these are present in most advanced nations, many factors that are unique to New Zealand make them even more important.

Because New Zealand is a relatively small country surrounded by ocean and blessed with numerous ports, most cities and towns have easy access to the sea. This facilitates both the importing of any necessary raw materials, as well as the exporting of finished products. Getting materials to and from the ports poses few problems because of the country's network of modern roads. Moreover, all cities, and even the smallest towns, have access to New Zealand's railways. Moving products from place to place is a simple matter in a small country like New Zealand that has efficient transportation systems.

A modern communication system is crucial to efficient business, and New Zealand offers high quality telephone and cellular systems. A business person in New Zealand takes for granted the same types of computer and communications networks that his or her counterpart in any other advanced nation enjoys. Modern communications and data systems enable companies to monitor inventory constantly and move products to markets smoothly.

The Banking System

Underlying any strong economic system is a country's banking system. During the past twenty years New Zealand's financial systems have changed rather dramatically to provide the services needed by a growing economy. Banks have become more diversified, sophisticated, and innovative with the services and programs they offer. During this period, banks have enjoyed the fruits of deregulation so that they can truly aid business in its expansion.

Two types of banks predominate in New Zealand: registered banks and international banks. The vast majority of banks in New Zealand are registered and governed by the Reserve Bank of New Zealand (RBNZ). The Reserve Bank of New Zealand Act of 1989 provides the Reserve Bank with the authority to register banks that adhere to specific criteria in the operation of their business. International banks also conduct their business as registered banks. They may be a branch of a parent bank or be a local bank. Registered banks offer the various services that an individual or business person would expect in any western country.

Other types of financial institutions include merchant banks and finance companies. Merchant banks offer services to corporations, handle investment portfolios, and assist companies in the process of acquisitions and mergers. Finance companies, on the other hand, offer their services mostly to individuals and small businesses. They offer loans and assistance to their clients for a variety of needs, with much of their lending being geared to the consumer.

Abundant Opportunities

Throughout New Zealand investment opportunities abound. While one may find these opportunities in both cities and towns, some regions are especially noteworthy.

One of these is Rotorua. Primarily known as a center for tourism, Rotorua has also emerged as a major site of forestry, agriculture, and most recently, retailing. Indeed, Rotorua is the country's leading tourism center and one of its major forestry regions. Located in the central part of the North Island, Rotorua is in an excellent position to expand upon its already significant economic base. As evidence of the region's focus upon economic growth and investment, the Rotorua District Council works closely with the New Zealand Association for Migration and Investment.

Investment opportunities are varied, although most are related to tourism, agriculture, retailing, or forestry. Because tourism is growing, retailing, frequently designed to meet the needs of tourists, is growing as well. In agriculture and forestry, there are many opportunities in the buying of forests and farms, as well as in industries and processes that provide services to these areas. Manufacturing is also growing in the region in response to the growth of farming and forestry. Production generally is related in some way to the processing of food and wood products. In addition, a small but vital and expanding industry of machinery manufacture offers unique investment opportunities, especially for machines that aid the production processes of the area's major industries.

Along with Rotorua, Waikato is another region that provides vast opportunities for investment. The region itself is made up mostly of rich, fertile farm and pasture land, while the region's main city, Hamilton, has grown into an industrial center.

Because of its fine pastures, Waikato is home to nearly 50% of New Zealand's horse-breeding industry. Clearly, for investors who wish to find a stake in horse breeding, Waikato is one of the first parts of New Zealand to explore. No less important because of the pastures is dairy farming, which offers opportunities not only in dairying but in support industries as well.

Hamilton, New Zealand's biggest inland city, has grown significantly in the past few decades to become a commercial center. It has an energetic population of about 100,000, is close to two main ports and an airport, and is linked to other parts of the country by road and rail. As the city grows, so will its need for skilled individuals who can provide the expertise and businesses it requires for the service of its people and established industries.

Hamilton is not only a center for business, however. Located in the city is the University of Waikato, one of New Zealand's major institutions for higher learning. Also in Hamilton is the Ruakura Agricultural Center, the country's largest agricultural research center, and the Meat Industry Research Institute of New Zealand, which is generally acknowledged as the country's foremost meat industry research center.

Along with its horse breeding, dairy farms, and industrial base, the Waikato region is also becoming known for tourism. The Waitomo Caves, breathtaking in their scope and beauty, attract more than a quarter of a million people each year. The region's west coast offers magnificent beaches and deep-sea fishing, while surfers rejoice in the waves off Raglan.

The Waikato region possesses fertile land, which is anchored by a growing city. The entire region offers a host of investment opportunities.

Yet another prime area for investment is Auckland. New Zealand's biggest city, Auckland offers investors opportunities of the kind they would find in virtually any large, modern city anywhere in the world — except that in New Zealand, the investors realize the rewards of everything else New Zealand offers: expanding economy, pleasant climate, friendly people, no pollution, no congestion, and certainly not nearly the level of crime that plagues other cities around the world.

Wellington is still another potential area for investment. New Zealand's capital city, Wellington is a place filled with excitement and energy. Being the seat of the country's government, the city is a center of commerce, educational services, social programs, and culture. It also provides the home for many corporations and government agencies.

The city is growing, and new enterprises are encouraged. Possessing one of the world's finest deep-water harbors, serviced by quality roads and railways, and at the center of New Zealand's state-of-the-art communications systems, Wellington is positioned for solid, steady growth in the future. Various business opportunities are available in both small and large companies that provide the services and products required by a modern capital city.

Wellington is also known as a cultural center. The city's population is descended from the original Maori, as well as Europeans, Chinese, Indians, and Samoans. Art and music gain much of their flavor from this diverse background, enhancing Wellington's rich culture.

These are not the only places in New Zealand that offer superior investment opportunities for both New Zealanders and newcomers alike. Following is a list of investment opportunities throughout the country. This is only a brief summary, and should by no means be thought of as listing all the investment opportunities in the country.

Investment Opportunities in the North Island

Northland: Whangarei, one of New Zealand's fastest growing cities, is becoming an important industrial center. Major industries and services include engineering, oil refining, ship-building, glass-making, and cement-making. Investment opportunities are available in these areas, as well as in support services.

Auckland: With its population nearing one million, Auckland offers boundless opportunities to investors. Just about every service found in every major city throughout the world is a potential investment for innovative entrepreneurs. A cultural center, shops, galleries, and theaters are located throughout the city. Recreation, especially boating, is an area offering excellent investment opportunities.

Coromandel Peninsula: Many artists and craftsmen live here, and there are investment opportunities in connection with tourism.

Bay of Plenty: Much of New Zealand's kiwifruit comes from this region. There is plenty of opportunity here as kiwifruit becomes a favorite throughout the world.

The Volcanic Plateau: This is the region around Rotorua. Tourism, forestry, agriculture, and a growing manufacturing base all offer major investment opportunities.

Waikato: A region of fertile farmlands and pastures, Waikato offers opportunities in dairy farming, fruit and vegetable farming, cattle raising, and horse breeding. The region's major city, Hamilton, is one of New Zealand's largest cities and offers a variety of opportunities associated with any growing city. The Waitomo Caves are a prime tourist site.

Taranaki: Onshore and offshore reserves of natural gas and oil provide exceptional opportunity for energy development. Egmont National Park is a major attraction for tourists.

Manawatu and Wanganui: The Wanganui River offers some of New Zealand's most spectacular scenery and is an important waterway for commerce and pleasure boaters.

The East Coast: A region of great geographical variety, the East Coast is sparsely populated. Urewera National Park is located in the region.

Wairarapa: While cattle graze in this region, the Wairarapa is primarily sheep country. Napier, one of the region's main cities, is a port, a center of commerce, and a resort. Hastings, the region's other major city that is located inland, is a commercial center that services the interior of the Wairarapa region. Both cities are vibrant, growing and offer countless investment opportunities.

Wellington: New Zealand's capital provides investment opportunities in business, the arts, and government-related services. A bustling, growing city, Wellington is filled with opportunities for the innovative.

Investment Opportunities in the South Island

Nelson: Enjoying one of the sunniest climates of New Zealand, Nelson is an important vacation spot, offering the myriad business opportunities that come with the tourist trade. Also because of its excellent weather, the region is a major producer of fruits. Farms and orchards are found throughout the area.

Marlborough: Marlborough shares Nelson's sunny climate, and while farming is an important part of the region's economy, so too is sheep grazing. Rural investments abound in Marlborough.

The West Coast: This region is best known for its history, in which gold played a prominent role, and also for its wondrous natural beauty, particularly its glaciers. Containing a population of only some 40,000, the region has plenty of room for expansion.

Canterbury: The plains of Canterbury provide some of New Zealand's best grazing land; sheep herding and its support industries are central to the region's economic activity. Canterbury also contains some of the country's highest peaks and is visited by countless skiers. Christchurch, Canterbury's principal city, is the largest city on the South Island. While the sheep industry remains important, over 30% of the city's employment is in manufacturing. The typical service industries essential to any modern bustling city also provide an assortment of investment opportunities.

Otago: Much of this region is occupied with sheep grazing. Near the coast, orchards are an important segment of the area's economy, although the mining of coal and production of hydroelectric power have grown in importance during the last few decades. The capital city of Otago is Dunedin. With a population of close to 100,000, Dunedin offers various business and investment opportunities. Along with its opportunities, Dunedin enjoys a low cost of living and an excellent lifestyle.

Southland: Inland areas of this region support sheep grazing, beef, and farming.

In seeking to start a business in New Zealand, one need not limit himself to the above. Because virtually all of the segments of New Zealand's economy are expanding, investment opportunities can be easily found in farming, grazing, service industries, energy, and manufacturing. A general rule of thumb for investors is to first look at the industries or fields with which they are by training or experience familiar. It is quite likely that they will be able to find ample investment opportunities in the areas of their expertise. Of course, for those who wish to start a new career or launch a new enterprise, opportunities are nearly boundless, limited only by one's vision for the future.

Chapter Twelve
Taxation

No matter where a person lives, in any industrialized country, he must pay taxes. The tax systems, however, vary from country to country, and quite obviously people pay different amounts of taxes depending on where they live. What is most important to the individual is that he pays his fair share and nothing more.

Today, unfortunately, many countries, in their attempts to pay for budget deficits, excessive social programs, and bureaucratic mismanagement that results in the wasting of tax dollars, must increase the tax rates levied on their citizens. In New Zealand, while the government recognizes the need for taxes, it also understands the burden that unfair taxation places on its citizens. As a result, New Zealand's tax system has been designed to be fair and equitable.

New Zealand's tax structure includes various types of taxes. The one that produces the most revenue for the government is the income tax. Other important taxes include those for fringe benefits and goods and services. It should be noted that New Zealand has no capital gains tax, although profits from some investments might be considered taxable income.

The Income Tax

Each year taxpayers must pay their income taxes. All income received by an individual during the taxable year — April 1 to

March 31 — is subject to income tax. People, companies, and unincorporated bodies that are bound together for the purpose of making a profit are all required to pay income taxes. The income tax is assessed on gross income, which includes several categories:

+ Business profits
+ Employment income
+ Profits earned on stocks or similar investments
+ Earnings-related compensation
+ Rents
+ Interest
+ Dividends
+ Royalties
+ Pensions

In addition, certain other types of profit-making are subject to income taxes, including:

+ Property other than land that is acquired for the purpose of resale, or sold with the result being profit.
+ Land, excepting residential or farmland, that is acquired for eventual resale, or sold by a dealer within 10 years of its original purchase. Also, land sold by a builder within 10 years of having made some type of improvement on it is subject to income tax. Other land deals are also affected by the 10-year limit, such as land sold because of zoning law changes or usage, or sold as part of a subdivision. Land that is sold at any time, which is part of a development or subdivision, and which has gained for the owner a profit because of increased value, is also subject to income tax.

Taxpayers (individuals and companies) are assessed tax on all their income while they are residents of New Zealand. While this includes income from overseas operations, a tax credit is permitted for taxes levied by foreign governments in cases where the foreign tax is similar to New Zealand income tax. However, the tax credit may not be greater than the taxes paid in New Zealand in the given tax year.

Nonresidents are responsible only for paying income tax on income they acquired in New Zealand. While this often means a direct profit on a business, it also includes the following:

♦ Any profits derived from the ownership of land.
♦ Any profits derived from acting as an employee or agent in New Zealand.
♦ Any profits derived from investments.
♦ Any interest earned on money lent in New Zealand.
♦ Any profits derived from contracts that operate in New Zealand.
♦ Royalties.

The definition of residency is important to taxpayers. According to New Zealand tax law, a resident is an individual who is present in New Zealand for more than 183 days (aggregate) during a 12-month period.

For some types of nonresident income, a flat-rate withholding tax is imposed. Interest, dividends, and royalties, as well as some types of contract payments and pay for consulting, come under this category.

Residency definitions for individuals and companies are somewhat different. A company is considered to be a resident if it is incorporated in New Zealand; if its central office is in the country; if its central management is in New Zealand; or if its directors maintain control in New Zealand.

While nonresident companies may be levied the nonresident withholding tax, they may be assessed an additional 5% over the normal company tax rate of 33% on all income where the nonresident withholding tax is not a final tax.

Tax Rates

New Zealand relies on a progressive tax system. Tax rates for individuals are 24% on income up to $30,875, and 33% on income over $30,875. (Note that individuals whose income is more than $30,875 pay only 24% on the first $30,875 of their income; only the income above $30,875 is taxed at a higher rate.) For resident companies the rate is a flat one of 33%; nonresident companies are most often taxed at a flat rate of 38%. Nonresident companies may be eligible for tax credits in some instances.

For most individuals, their employers deduct their taxes from salaries or wages and submit them to the Inland Revenue Department monthly. In some cases tax monies may be submitted biweekly. This system is called the PAYE. The amount deducted is calculated in advance, based on the annualized income of the taxpayer. For income earned that does not result from a typical employer/employee relationship, tax deductions are made from payments received.

For companies and the self-employed, payment of provisional taxes is required, usually in three installments that are based on the income of the previous year. There are some exceptions to this, however. Taxpayers who are unlikely to pay more than $2,500 income tax for the year are not generally required to pay the provisional taxes. Nonresidents who do not have a permanent establishment in New Zealand are not required to pay provisional taxes either.

The GST — Goods and Services Tax

The GST is a value-added tax on most transactions that involve the supplying of goods and services. The rate of the GST is 12.5%. Although it is paid by the supplier, it is typically added to the cost of the product and is then passed along to the buyer. Only suppliers whose taxable supplies surpass $30,000 per year must register for the GST.

Some suppliers are exempt. For example, the supply of financial services does not need to be registered for the GST. Another example is the sale of an operating business. Even though the sale might include various supplies, the GST in this case would be zero-rated.

GST is paid to the Inland Revenue Department in installments. Depending on the volume of the business, installments may be required monthly, bimonthly, or semiannually.

The Fringe Benefit Tax

The Fringe Benefit Tax (FBT) is paid by employers on the value of many non-cash benefits they give to their employees. Examples include low-interest loans, motor vehicles, the use of company equipment, and similar amenities. The FBT rate is 49% deductible.

Deductions and Depreciation

Deductions are permitted for those expenditures which are incurred in the gaining or producing of income, or for the typical costs incurred in the operation of a business. New Zealand tax law does not allow deductions for losses on capital.

Depreciation is permitted on buildings and facilities, machinery, and equipment typically used to produce income. The Commissioner of Inland Revenue sets the depreciation tax rates in the form of prescribed scales. The rates for depreciation are usually set on a diminishing value basis, except for buildings which, depending on kind, are depreciable between 1% and 2.5% of the cost price.

Interest and Dividends

The tax rules regarding interest and dividends are rather broad. A withholding tax of 24% is usually required on interest payments, while a withholding tax of 33% is required in most cases on dividends. In the case of nonresidents, the withholding tax for interest is 15% and for dividends it is 30%. For some taxpayers these rates are reduced because of double-tax treaties that New Zealand has entered into with other nations.

Tax Treaties

New Zealand has signed double-tax treaties with several other countries. The results of these treaties may reduce the amount of total tax an individual or company might have to pay. Tax treaties exist between New Zealand and the following nations:

United States	Australia	Japan
Sweden	West Germany	The Netherlands
Great Britain	Switzerland	Italy
Belgium	Norway	Finland
Ireland	France	Canada
Denmark	Fiji	China
Indonesia	India	Singapore
Republic of Korea	The Philippines	Malaysia

Individual Income Taxes

The payment rate for individual income taxes is dependent upon a person's residence. Residents and nonresidents are subject to slightly different tax code regulations and statutes. Thus, the definition of "residence" is important.

In New Zealand, under the tax law, an individual is considered to be a resident if any of the following conditions are met:

♦ The individual maintains a permanent residence in the country. The person may have residences in other countries, but as long as he or she maintains a residence in New Zealand, he or she is considered to be a resident.
♦ The individual is present in the country for more than 183 aggregate days in any twelve-month period.

♦ The individual is unable to be in the country, because he or she is in the service of the government.

An individual will be considered to be a nonresident if the following conditions are met:

♦ The individual is absent from New Zealand for an aggregate 325 days in any twelve-month period. This assumes that he does not maintain a permanent residency, and that he is not working for the government outside of the country.

For taxpayers who are residents of two countries, and who might suffer from double-taxation, the question of double-taxation is settled through the provisions of any existing tax treaties. Attempts are generally made to reduce or eliminate the burden of double-taxation.

Generally, all income is subject to income taxes. This includes wages, salaries, interest, money from rental properties, and royalties.

Employees who earn wages or salaries are a part of the PAYE tax-deduction system. Their employers deduct the appropriate taxes on the payments they make to their employees. The employers submit the deductions to the Inland Revenue Department (IRD) either monthly or bimonthly, depending upon the company and amount of the deductions.

The system is much like the one used in the United States by the Internal Revenue Service (IRS). The deducted taxes are by no means final. They are a payment that is adjusted at the end of the tax year, depending upon an employee's overall earnings. When too much money has been deducted, the employee receives a tax refund at the end of the year; in cases where not enough money has been deducted, the employee must pay the additional amount required.

On some jobs, employers offer their employees various types of allowances, commonly called "fringe benefits" in the United States. Depending on the type of allowance, it may or may not be taxable.

For example, an allowance that is paid to an employee that he uses for an unrelated job expense would be considered remuneration and would likely be taxable. Conversely, an allowance that reimburses a worker for a job-related expense that the employee originally paid would not be taxable.

In most cases, nonresident employees pay the same taxes as do their resident counterparts. However, nonresident employees are also subject to nonresident withholding taxes on interest, dividends, and royalties.

Although individuals may not claim deductions against employment income, deductions for business expenses are permitted. Individuals may claim certain losses, and may carry them forward from a previous year to offset current taxes.

Business and Taxes

Owners and managers of companies in New Zealand must be knowledgeable regarding the tax requirements that will affect their business. New Zealand tax law defines a company in a rather broad sense.

Simply put, any corporate body, which has been incorporated in New Zealand, or elsewhere but is doing business in New Zealand, is subject to New Zealand's business taxes. Any company incorporated under the Companies Act is subject to New Zealand's corporate taxes. In recent years, the definition has been extended to include unit trusts, incorporated societies, credit unions, and local or public authorities.

Resident companies must pay taxes on all income, whether that income is derived from New Zealand or elsewhere. Nonresident companies, however, are subject to taxes only on the income that is a result of their operations in New Zealand. This is obviously an advantage for nonresident companies, which the tax code encourages. After all, even when a company enjoys nonresident status, it most often employs New Zealanders in its domestic operations and still pays taxes on income that is a result of New Zealand business.

Nonresident companies pay taxes at a higher rate, 38%, as compared to the rate of 33% for resident public and private companies. This higher rate is somewhat offset by the fact that only New Zealand income is taxed. Also, in some cases, nonresident companies may apply for and be granted tax rebates.

Business Deductions

Companies are entitled to a variety of deductions in the normal course of doing business. Following are some of the more important possible deductions available:

♦ Typical expenses related to business operations.
♦ Decrease in the value of stocks.
♦ Costs of patents.
♦ Contributions to employee benefits programs.
♦ Charitable gifts and contributions.
♦ Depreciation on buildings, equipment, and fixed assets.

In some cases deductions are required to be apportioned between assessable and nonassessable income. Also, in the case of materials purchased for production but not used in the given tax year, the deductions that would normally result from such purchases may need to be adjusted.

Business Losses

When a company incurs losses in a given year, it may carry those losses forward to another income year where they may be used to offset a future profit. However, this can only be done if the control and shareholding in the company continues at a level of 40% or more. Losses may also be transferred between companies, but only if they qualify to be carried forward to upcoming years.

Stocks and Taxes

The value of stocks for tax purposes may be set at cost, the market price, or replacement price. The decided value is optional. For companies that have a high proportion of common shareholding, special tax provisions apply. In cases where shareholders are other companies, stock ownership falls back to the individual owner of the stock. Many companies in New Zealand offer stocks to potential investors.

The Imputation Credit Account

New Zealand companies must institute Imputation Credit Accounts (ICA). The purpose of the account is to maintain a record of the tax a company has paid, adjusted by imputation credits that have been distributed to shareholders. The aim of this system is to eliminate the double taxation that occurs when a company's profits are taxed, only to be followed by shareholders' profits (in the form of dividends) being taxed. Not only does the company benefit from imputation credits, but shareholders, too, may receive tax credits for allotted imputation credits. The overall result of the Imputation Credit Account is to make sure that the income obtained through a company is not subject to being taxed twice.

There are limitations to the Imputation Credit Account, however. For example, the ICA is available only to resident companies. Nonresident shareholders are not entitled to use the ICA as a means of reducing or offsetting any taxes. Although nonresidents are not able to use the ICA, in many cases they are able to use withholding payment credits to offset nonresident withholding tax requirements.

Special Considerations — Partnerships, Joint Ventures, and Trusts

Partnerships, joint ventures, and trusts enjoy special considerations under New Zealand's tax laws. Investors considering them should review the various advantages and disadvantages of each.

Although partnerships must file an annual return of income, the actual partnership is not viewed as an individual and is therefore not taxed. The purpose of the return is to record income and its disbursement among the partners. The members of the partnership are then taxed on the income they derive from the partnership, as well as any other income they may earn from other sources. The income that partners receive from the partnership is determined by the agreement of the partnership, usually written during the formation of the partnership. Any losses are determined in the same manner. In cases where a partner withdraws from the partnership, his or her stock or share is accounted at market value. Should the partnership continue, the overall value of the partnership, its income and any losses, is adjusted accordingly.

Partnerships may conduct business under the structure of a joint venture. However, joint ventures may also be entered into by corporations or a combination of partnerships and corporations. Joint ventures offer various tax advantages and disadvantages, depending on how they are initially structured. In most cases, the members of the joint venture will be assessed taxes based upon their overall income.

Like partnerships and joint ventures, trusts offer investors both opportunities and drawbacks. The terms "qualifying" and "non-qualifying" are important in determining the potential advantages a trust may have to one's investment strategies. Residence is also important.

Beneficiary income is included in the assessable income of an individual. The astute investor will review the various tax options open to him and select the one that best fits his needs.

A Fair Tax Code

While it is certainly true that no one likes to pay taxes, it is also true that taxes are necessary for the operation and maintenance of government. Most people realize the need for taxes, but become frustrated and angry when they see their taxes squandered on foolish programs or wasted through negligence, fraud, poor accounting procedures, or when they feel that their tax burden is excessive.

Unlike the tax codes of many advanced nations, the tax laws of New Zealand are designed to ensure the country's growth. Care has been taken that business is encouraged rather than burdened by taxes, and that individuals feel that the money they pay in taxes goes to worthwhile programs.

Chapter Thirteen
Deciding to Immigrate

It is a major decision to move to another country. In the case of immigrating to New Zealand, the decision is made much easier when one realizes that he is moving to a land where he will in all likelihood enjoy a far better lifestyle.

New Zealand clearly offers many advantages to those considering moving to the country. It is a prosperous nation where the opportunities that await an individual are limited only by that person's creativity and drive. It is a clean country; New Zealanders cherish their environment and are aware of how fragile any environment can be. It is a place of breathtaking beauty where the mountains and sea are within easy access from almost anywhere. It is a land that offers all of the modern amenities that people from advanced nations have come to expect. Finally, compared to many other industrialized nations, New Zealand is relatively crime-free, although, as is the case all over the world, crime is increasing.

Without question, New Zealand has countless desirable attributes. Aside from its scenery, political neutrality, and exceptional lifestyle, the country has made substantial efforts to attract foreign investment and immigrants. Taxes tend to be lower than the taxes of European countries and roughly equal to those in the United States. New Zealand actively encourages entrepreneurs and investors to come to their country.

Once you have made your decision, there are many factors of which you need to be aware. That is the purpose of this chapter —

to offer you the basic information you will need to know in order that your move to New Zealand is efficient, smooth, and enjoyable.

Passports and Visas

Whether you are traveling to New Zealand with the intention to stay or just visit, you will need a passport. Furthermore, the passport must be valid for a minimum of three months after the date you plan to leave New Zealand.

Visas are not required for travelers from most countries. However, if you have any questions, you may consult the New Zealand Immigration Service, P.O. Box 4130, Wellington, New Zealand.

Upon your arrival in New Zealand, you will be required to complete an arrival card. This is a short formality, and need not be a concern.

Of course, there are many agencies and companies that provide consultation services for immigrants. Such organizations can handle any paperwork and answer all questions, as well as help in finding a home, setting up a business, or making investments. Such organizations will be covered in the next chapter.

Money

New Zealand's currency is based on dollars and cents. Coins represent values of 5¢, 10¢, 20¢, 50¢, $1, and $2. Paper denominations come in values of $5, $10, $20, $50, and $100.

Of course, a New Zealand dollar is not equal in value to a U.S. dollar. In December 1995, one New Zealand dollar was worth approximately 66 U.S. cents. Conversely, one U.S. dollar brought 1.54 New Zealand dollars in exchange.

Most major credit cards are accepted throughout the country. Those used most commonly include American Express, Master-Card, Visa, and Diners Club.

Travelers checks are also commonly accepted. Most banks, major hotels, and even some major stores regularly cash travelers checks.

New Zealand currency, (Top: $5 bill, coins from left:
50¢, $2, $1, 10¢, 5¢).

Should you need the services of a bank, most are open Monday through Friday. Some banks maintain branches at the international airports where they provide foreign exchange services seven days a week.

Should you be interested in shopping, you have a variety of choices. You can choose from stores in the city, suburban shopping malls, or visit some of the rural areas where many specialty shops can be found. Most stores are open from 9 a.m. until 5 p.m. Monday through Friday, although many are open longer, especially shopping centers and malls. Convenience stores are often open seven days per week. If you are interested in shopping in duty-free stores, you can find these in major cities and at airports.

Planning Your Trip

For most people, the best way to come to New Zealand is by air. The country has international airports in Auckland, Wellington, and Christchurch. Depending on the city from which you leave, flight times vary considerably. Following are some examples; note that flight times are estimates:

Paris: 26 hours	Hong Kong: 11 hours
London: 26 hours	Los Angeles: 12 hours
New Delhi: 18 hours	Seoul: 13 hours
Singapore: 10 hours	Tokyo: 10½ hours

When planning travel schedules, it is worthwhile to remember that New Zealand lies in the southern hemisphere, close to the International Date Line. It is therefore 12 hours ahead of Greenwich Mean Time. Its seasons are the opposite of those in the northern hemisphere.

While the climate does vary somewhat from region to region, in general, New Zealand enjoys a year-round growing season. Much of the country experiences moderate to regular rainfall and temperatures that are mild (December to March) to somewhat cool, or cold in a few areas (June to September).

Since agriculture is so important to New Zealand, and great efforts are made to keep the country free from diseases that strike plants and animals, the importation of some animals and plants (and plant materials) are regulated. Should you intend to take animals or plants into the country, you will need to complete the proper forms before your arrival. You may contact the Ministry of Agriculture and Fisheries, P.O. Box 2526, Wellington, New Zealand, for more information.

Along with the regulations regarding agriculture, you need to be aware of various customs allowances when traveling to New Zealand. Visitors of 17 years of age and older, together with their personal effects, are allowed goods whose value totals $NZ 700 free of duty and the Goods and Services Tax (GST). Goods whose value totals more than that may be subject to duty and GST; however, no payment is necessary unless the amount to be collected is $50 or more. Visitors may obtain more information regarding goods and duty fees and GST by contacting The Controller of Customs, P.O. Box 11-746, Wellington, New Zealand. A variety of informational publications is available from The Controller of Customs. Usually, if you move to New Zealand with the intention of making it your home, thereby taking up immediate residency, duty fees and GST may be waived.

In addition to personal effects and goods, cigarettes, cigars, tobacco, alcoholic beverages, and motor vehicles are regulated as noted below:

- To remain free of duty fees and GST, not more than 200 cigarettes, or 250 grams of tobacco, or 50 cigars, or a mixture of all three that totals a weight of 250 grams or less may be brought into the country.
- To remain free of duty and GST, not more than 4.5 liters of wine, or 4.5 liters of beer, and one bottle of spirits or liqueur that contains 1,125 ml or less may be brought into the country.
- The importation of motor vehicles is regulated. It is advisable to consult The Controller of Customs at the above address regarding the particular vehicle you would like to bring into the country.

An additional note on motor vehicles should you wish to rent a car while in the country — while New Zealand maintains reciprocal driving rights with most countries, most rental car companies will require that you have obtained an International Driving Permit. Most people, however, can drive private vehicles using their driver's license from their own country. Typically, the license will be considered valid until June 30, which is the end of the licensing year. (For more information on driving in New Zealand, see the section in Chapter 16, "Driving and Cars.")

A Few Final Things to Know

When traveling to New Zealand, keep in mind the climate and time of year. Remember that seacoast and mountains are often in easy access to each other and weather conditions between the two places can vary.

Since most places in New Zealand follow a rather casual lifestyle, formal attire is seldom necessary. Casual clothing is generally fine even for quality restaurants.

When you are in New Zealand, you are seldom far from a phone. All of the country has high quality telephone service, and much of the country has access to cellular service.

Just as it is easy to stay in touch with others by phone, you can easily remain in touch with world and local events. Every city has at least one daily newspaper, radio stations, and is in receiving range of television broadcasts.

Should you need to use the mail service, post offices in the country are usually open from 8:30 a.m. to 5 p.m. Monday through Friday. You may mail letters and packages locally, nationally, and internationally.

Following is a brief listing of some important facts for travelers to New Zealand:

Geography: New Zealand is about the size of Great Britain. Lying in the southern hemisphere, it is southeast of Australia. The country is graced with excellent beaches, spectacular mountains, glaciers, volcanoes, countless lakes, and breathtaking scenery.

Climate: Mild in summer to cool and somewhat cold in winter. Moderate to regular rainfall. Year-round growing season.

Population: About 3.3 million, mostly of English descent. Slightly over 10% of the people have descended from the original Maori inhabitants.

Language: English for most of the people. Maori is also recognized as an official language.

Economy: Mostly agriculture-based, although manufacturing, high-tech products, geothermal, natural gas, and hydroelectric energy are becoming increasingly important. Shopping malls are evidence of a growing consumer segment of the economy.

Tax Structure: Roughly equivalent to that of the United States; not as burdensome as most of the European countries.

Communications: A highly modern system that is rapidly incorporating digital and cellular technologies into its basic framework.

Immigration Policy: Encourages the immigration of people who can bring knowledge, business expertise, and capital to the country.

New Zealand is perhaps the only country today in which opportunities for those willing to work hard are virtually unlimited. It is a place where dreams can be turned into reality.

Chapter 14
Making the Move

For anyone who has moved into a new home, even if it is just around the block, the actual move can be a trying, difficult experience. When moving to another country, all of the potential pitfalls increase. Effective research and planning can avoid those pitfalls and make even a move halfway around the world go smoothly. Instead of it being a worrisome experience, your move, if planned properly, can be a time of happy anticipation and the beginning of a new life.

Thorough planning is crucial. Reread and study this book carefully, as well as other sources that can give you important insights about New Zealand.

Pay close attention to the various regions. Where do you think you would be most comfortable? Do you enjoy an urban lifestyle? If you do, perhaps Auckland would be a good choice. Do you enjoy a suburban or rural setting? New Zealand offers a variety of regions that, while still offering all the good things that are New Zealand, also offer diversity. Do you prefer to live near the sea or in the mountains? Are you a skier or a swimmer? Do you have school-age children? If yes, be sure to check into the schools in the areas you are considering for a home. It might prove helpful to list on a sheet of paper all the factors that you desire in a new home, and then match them against several areas of the country that you are considering settling in.

Another major factor, of course, is a region's economy. Do you plan to start a business? Are you interested in investing in a particular type of company? Will you be working as a consultant, offering your expertise to many different businesses? Compare the various cities and regions and determine which ones offer you the most opportunity. You should go where your talents and experience are most likely to have an impact and where you are likely to enjoy the greatest economic advantages.

If possible, you might wish to visit New Zealand and travel through the country. Not only will this help to acquaint you with the country's characteristics and peculiarities, but it will permit you a firsthand look at potential sites where you might consider moving. No books or brochures can provide you with such personal experience. If you are able to arrange a trip to New Zealand, be sure to check business opportunities, too. Contacts you make now can prove quite beneficial later.

There are many factors to consider when relocating to another country. You will be leaving your current home, your family, friends, career, and accustomed lifestyle for a new land that will hold many new experiences.

Nevertheless, you must realize that New Zealand is a land populated by immigrants. When the Europeans first came to the country, they met the Maori inhabitants, who had come to New Zealand some 600 years before them. While some people feel comfortable in making such a move by themselves, others feel more secure working with an immigration consultant who can help them with the many questions they will have.

Immigration Consultants

Immigrating to a new country is a major step in one's life. For most people, it is the most important career or lifestyle decision they will make. For many, having someone to guide them through the process can be enormously helpful.

How does one select an immigration consultant? Ideally, the best way is through someone who has used the consultant for his or her own move to New Zealand. An endorsement from someone you know and trust is the best kind of recommendation.

If you don't know of anyone who has used an immigration consultant, you should check for a consultant's membership in the New Zealand Association for Migration and Investment (NZAMI). Founded in 1989, the purpose of NZAMI is to act as the professional organization that oversees the standards by which immigration consultants conduct their business. Although NZAMI was originally founded by consulting firms, membership in the body has been broadened and now includes banks, legal firms, and accounting firms.

NZAMI requires its members to adhere to a strict Code of Ethics. Members may not permit the influence of nationality, race, religion, or politics to affect any dealings with clients; they may not provide false information; they may not exert any pressure on clients for their own financial gain; members will agree in advance with their clients on a fee; member firms will not disclose confidential information regarding their clients without the prior consent of the client. These are just some of the major highlights of the Code of Ethics that governs immigration consultants who are members of NZAMI.

NZAMI also works closely with the New Zealand government. Indeed, because of the organization's advice and influence, the government, in recent years, has revised some of its regulations regarding immigration to make it easier for newcomers to settle in New Zealand. The overall purpose of these policies is to attract the talent and skills that will aid the country's economic and social growth.

Many government officials and planners believe that it is vital for New Zealand to increase its population. They feel that the country's 3.3 million citizens are too small in number to achieve a self-sustaining economy. Immigration would clearly be a major boost to the economy over the long term. Coupled with New Zealand's strength in exporting, immigration is considered to be the key to New Zealand's future. (It should be noted, though, that popular opposition to Asian immigration to New Zealand is growing, and this may eventually force the government to revise its present immigration policies.)

NZAMI not only monitors the services in the field of immigration, but provides services in the area of investments for immigrants as well. Companies and organizations that are members of NZAMI are encouraged to help immigrants find the investments that are most in line with their personal financial goals.

Should you wish to contact NZAMI, you may do so through mail or by phone. Write: The Secretary, New Zealand Association for Migration and Investment, Inc., P.O. Box 518, Tauranga, New Zealand. Phone: 64-7-578-1883. Fax: 64-7-578-2555.

Immigrants are advised to avoid any immigration consulting firm that is not a member of NZAMI. In addition, they are advised to avoid any of the offshore consulting services that purport to know New Zealand as well as those companies established in the nation. Offshore firms simply cannot provide the same expertise or experience as those firms which are a part of New Zealand's everyday life. Moreover, while overseas firms may be able to arrange the details of the move to New Zealand, they are often unable or unwilling to address problems or questions that arise afterward.

Following are some important questions you should ask before committing yourself to any immigration consulting firm:

- Is the organization a member of NZAMI? Does it adhere to the professional standards developed and supported by NZAMI?
- Is the consulting firm based in New Zealand? Are its representatives New Zealanders?
- How long has the firm been in business? How much experience in guiding immigrants do its representatives have?

♦ Does your representative possess experience in the area of your career? Can he or she guide you in starting a business or beginning a new career?
♦ Do you feel comfortable with your representative? Do you feel that he or she is knowledgeable? Does he or she seem willing to answer all of your questions? Does he or she seem sympathetic to your concerns?
♦ Does the firm provide all of the services you will need? Can it help with housing? Moving? Paperwork?
♦ Are the firm's fees reasonable? Does it provide any guarantees?

Since arriving on New Zealand soil is only the first part of becoming a citizen, you should select an immigration consulting firm that offers services well beyond the mere move. Member companies of NZAMI typically provide a full range of services. Not only do they help with establishing a new home but they aid newcomers in establishing themselves within their new communities. This may include help in securing a home, setting up a business or beginning a new career, or helping the family to adapt to their new lifestyle.

It is advisable to check several immigration consulting firms before making your final choice. Weigh the strengths and weaknesses of each against the others. Only then should you select the firm that best suits your individual needs.

Obtaining a Moving Firm

Just as planning ahead of time can make your overall move to New Zealand safe and trouble-free, planning can help make your actual move — the transporting of your possessions to New Zealand — easier. No one enjoys their move anywhere if they arrive and their possessions don't. Even worse is when their possessions arrive damaged.

One of the most important steps you should take when planning your move is to decide which of your "things" you won't be taking with you. Some items — major appliances and big pieces of furniture — may not be practical to move, especially if they are relatively old. You can buy new ones in New Zealand. It may be a waste of time moving electric appliances to New Zealand, where the current is 230/240 volts, 50 hertz. A good example: it makes little sense to move a ten-year-old air-conditioner. For such items, try negotiating them into the sale price of your home. If the new owners are not interested in them, run an advertisement in the local newspaper. For small items, hold a garage or yard sale. Many people sell items when moving. Not only do they reduce the amount of materials they need to move, but they gain extra cash as well.

In the past, some immigrants brought their cars to New Zealand. The reason then was simple, because it could be rather expensive to buy the car of one's choice in the country due to import taxes and tariffs. Those taxes and tariffs have been eliminated or reduced, making it much easier now to buy various models of cars. Indeed, it is usually easier to buy a car in the country than to bring your own from your former land.

When moving your possessions, it is essential that you enlist the services of an international mover who has a solid reputation and maintains branches in New Zealand. Make sure that the mover you choose is a member of international moving industry organizations; this will assure you that the company is experienced and competent. Belonging to either the Bar or FIDI, two international organizations, requires that member companies adhere to strict standards of operations. Companies that belong to either or both organizations can be counted on to be professional and courteous.

In considering a moving company, you should eliminate companies that:

1. Do not maintain branch offices in New Zealand.
2. Subcontract packing.
3. Subcontract shipping.

In other words, when you select a company to move your possessions, that company, and only that company, should be held responsible for the task. When a company subcontracts any parts of the move, there is a greater chance for mistakes and damage. Moreover, if a company does not maintain a branch in New Zealand, preferably close to the city or region you are moving to, it is less likely to be able to make your move as smooth as possible. A company that does have New Zealand branches is more likely to know the routes and procedures that will enable it to move your possessions efficiently and safely. Companies that maintain branches in New Zealand are also more likely to be able to provide you with important information regarding your move. They can advise you on meeting customs requirements and provide you with other pertinent information that you will need to know.

Companies that handle their own shipping and that have experience in moving families to New Zealand are more likely to understand and maintain international packing and shipping standards, ensure more effective shipping while enroute, and possess better capabilities to track their shipments. All of this, of course, results in more peace of mind for you.

Before making your final decision on any moving company, ask for a list of former clients whom you might contact, or written testimonials from prior customers. A solid recommendation from a previously satisfied customer can often put any last worries you may have to rest. On the other hand, if the company cannot furnish you with such a list or testimonials, or is reluctant to do so, you may do well to consider another company.

The importance of choosing a moving company that can help you transfer your property smoothly, efficiently, and competently cannot be overemphasized. (See the following checklist.) When you feel comfortable with your moving company, and have confidence that they will do a professional job, not only will you have fewer worries but you will be able to focus your attention on other aspects of your move.

A Checklist for Moving to New Zealand

Using the following checklist can make your move to New Zealand safe and efficient.

☐ Make sure that family members have current passports. If you or others don't have one, apply for it. Be sure to include photos.

☐ If you intend to use the services of an immigration consultant, begin making your inquiries well in advance. Be sure that the individual or company you select is a member of NZAMI.

☐ Begin the search for a moving company in advance. Remember to select one with international moving experience and that maintains branches in New Zealand. Testimonials and recommendations from former customers can help you make your final decision.

☐ Complete the necessary documentation that will be required for your entry into New Zealand. (When you move, be sure that you keep such materials handy — a personal travel bag is a good idea — so that you can present them or refer to them as needed.)

☐ Begin attending to the sale of your old home and possessions.

☐ Attend to any financial and legal concerns. For many immigrants, old bills can be paid once the house is sold. Attend to any tax matters that may be pertinent.

☐ Carefully determine which possessions you will take with you and which ones you will sell or leave behind. In general, it doesn't make sense to take major appliances or even automobiles, as it is often easier to buy new ones in New Zealand.

☐ Contact your moving company and make the final arrangements.

☐ Obtain all personal records and documents — birth certificates, marriage licenses, medical records, school records for children, etc. Such personal information can be helpful in settling into your new lifestyle.

☐ Inform your work, children's schools, associates, friends, and relatives of your upcoming move. Attend to any necessary transfers or paperwork, for example, signing your children out of school. Make certain that the necessary people and agencies have your new address and phone number (if you have already obtained the phone number).

☐ Doublecheck your plans so far. Contact your immigration consultant (if you have one), and your moving company to make certain that everything is set and ready to go. Pose any questions you may have. Now is the time to settle any outstanding issues and clear up any confusion.

☐ Throw out or recycle items that you are not planning to take with you. (If you are discarding several items, you might start doing this a few weeks ahead of time.)

☐ On the day of moving, confer with your moving company to minimize confusion. Make certain that the movers are aware of everything that has to be moved.

☐ Doublecheck all paperwork and documentation.

☐ Make certain that everything that is to be moved is clean, dry, and ready to be packed. If you are taking major appliances with you, have a service technician come and prepare them for shipment.

☐ Be available to the moving crew. If you can't be there, appoint someone you trust who will be. This will help ensure that your possessions will be moved properly. It is often a good idea to walk the supervisor through the house and point out everything that is to go. This tends to reduce any confusion and helps ensure that everything that is supposed to be packed and shipped actually is.

☐ Don't try to help the movers pack or move your items. Leave everything where it normally is. Dishes should be left in the cabinets, pictures should be on the walls, silverware should be left in its drawers. The movers will pack them accordingly.

☐ Before the movers leave, walk through the house, garage, cellar, etc., and make certain that everything that was supposed to go was actually packed.

☐ Before the movers leave, check once more to ensure that they have the correct shipping address, as well as a phone number to contact you.

☐ Before leaving the house, make sure that you have all of your personal belongings and travel bags.

Chapter 15
Becoming a New Zealand Citizen

The New Zealand government encourages immigration. As noted earlier, most New Zealanders are in basic agreement on the benefits of immigration, most importantly to the growth of the country's economy. Nevertheless, despite their encouragement of new citizens, New Zealanders are well aware of the need to attract talented and experienced people who will not only enjoy all that New Zealand offers, but will be an asset to the nation as well.

To ensure that immigrants — and potential new citizens — will bring with them the skills and assets the country needs, the government has established guidelines to help people determine if they may be eligible for residence in New Zealand. Applications may be submitted under one of four basic categories: General Skills, Business Investor, Family, and Humanitarian.

The General Skills Category

This category, as its name implies, covers various areas of application for residence. Applicants are awarded points under factors such as employability, including work experience and job qualifications, age, and settlement factors, which include such things as settlement funds, investment funds, the applicant's being sponsored by a New Zealand citizen or organization, and an offer of skilled employment. Note that if you are applying under the

General Skills Category, you are expected to read, understand, and speak English. You will be required to conduct a conversation using English.

Employability is perhaps one of the most important factors under the General Skills Category. You can be awarded points as follows:

- Degree, diploma or trade certificate – 10 points
- Advanced qualification of a minimum of 4 years duration – 11 points
- Masters degree or higher – 12 points

If a person only holds a high school degree they cannot be considered under this category.

The above factors have some important restrictions. An applicant can obtain points for only one qualification; areas of study not fully completed are unacceptable; any qualification must be comparable to a similar New Zealand qualification.

Work experience is another important factor. For every two years of completed work experience, applicants can obtain one point. This is limited to a total of 10 points, however. If you have eight years work experience, for example, you will gain 4 points. The following restrictions apply regarding work experience:

- You may only score points for work experience if it is continuous, sound, and relevant to your qualifications; in other words, your work experience must be related to any degrees or training you received from schooling.
- The work experience must be in an approved occupation. An approved occupation is an occupation that is considered skilled in New Zealand and is listed in the New Zealand Immigration Service's Register of Approved Occupations. (In order to obtain points in this area, an applicant must have at least five years of experience in an approved occupation.)

A job offer also carries weight as an employability factor. You can be allocated 5 points if you receive a job offer from a New Zealand employer that is:

♦ Full time and;
♦ Permanent and;
♦ Current at the time of your application and at the time you are issued with a residence visa or permit and;
♦ Relevant to the qualifications that you are claiming points for.

If you are claiming points for a job offer in an occupation where registration is required by law in New Zealand, registration must be gained before points will be awarded.

Age is another factor under the General Skills Category. The age that your points will be based on is your age at the time you submit your application. Applicants over age 56 are not eligible for approval under the General Skills Category. Points are awarded for age as per the following:

♦ 18 – 24 years – 8 points
♦ 25 – 29 years – 10 points
♦ 30 – 34 years – 8 points
♦ 35 – 39 years – 6 points
♦ 40 – 44 years – 4 points
♦ 45 – 49 years – 2 points
♦ 50 – 55 years – 0 points.

Other important issues, called Settlement Factors, fall under the General Skills Category. It is possible to obtain a maximum of 7 points in this category, as follows:

♦ Settlement funds in the equivalent of $NZ 100,000 — 1 point (Settlement funds refer to assets such as the value of a house, cash, shares of stock, etc., less any debts.)
♦ For every $100,000 in investment funds transferred to New Zealand (up to $NZ200,000) — 1 point, maximum 2 points. (To gain the points under investment funds, you must have the funds,

between $100,000 and $200,000, transferred to New Zealand and invested in the country for at least two years. The investments must be invested in a way that provides a commercial return on the investment; the funds may not be invested for items of personal use. You need not transfer your funds to New Zealand until your application has been approved in principle.)

+ Spouse's qualifications can result in points. A spouse's degree, diploma, or trade certificate of a minimum of three years' duration is worth 1 point. A spouse's advanced qualification, master's degree or higher of a minimum of four years' duration is worth 2 points.

+ You can also score points for the lawful work experience you gain in New Zealand that is related to the qualification you are claiming points for, and shows that you were consistently a good employee. You can claim 1 point for every complete year, but only a maximum of 2 points are allowed.

+ Family sponsorship also results in an allocation of points. Your family sponsor must be 17 years of age or over; a New Zealand citizen or resident; have been lawfully and permanently living in New Zealand for at least three years, and: a parent, brother, sister, or child of the principal applicant or the principal applicant's spouse. If your family member undertakes to be your sponsor, they are responsible for providing information and advice about settling in New Zealand, and, if necessary, ensuring that accommodation is available to you for up to 12 months from your date of arrival in New Zealand. 3 points can be allocated if the family sponsor meets the requirements.

If you achieve a total of less than 24 points, you are not likely to qualify for residence in New Zealand under the General Skills Category.

Business Investor Category

The Business Investor Category is designed to ensure that those with high quality business skills can gain entrance to New Zealand. Generally, they are also expected to invest business funds in New Zealand. All applicants are expected to be proficient in the English language.

Points are allocated for business experience that the applicant has gained from owning or managing a lawful business enterprise or senior management experience in a lawful business enterprise, at the rate of 30 hours or more per week (those with fewer than 30 hours per week may be awarded points on a pro rata basis). The applicant can claim 1 point for each completed four-year period of business, up to a maximum of 5 points.

A "qualification" can also result in the allocation of points. A degree, diploma or certificate of a minimum of three years' duration (all of which must be comparable to a similar New Zealand qualification) is worth 1 point. An advanced qualification, master's degree or higher of a minimum of four years' duration is worth 2 points.

Accumulated earnings, funds and assets that were earned directly through your business experience in a lawful business enterprise and which will be invested in New Zealand for at least two years in an investment capable of providing a commercial return are also worth points. The funds must be owned wholly by the principal applicant or jointly with the principal applicant's spouse. The funds need not be transferred to New Zealand until your application has been approved in principle. At least 1 point for accumulated earnings funds must be scored when applying under the Business Investor Category, or your application cannot be approved.

Points are scored as follows:

- NZ$750,000 – 1 point
- NZ$1,000,000 – 2 points
- NZ$1,250,000 – 3 points
- NZ$1,500,000 – 4 points

- NZ$1,750,000 – 5 points
- NZ$2,000,000 – 6 points
- NZ$2,250,000 – 7 points
- NZ$2,500,000 – 8 points
- NZ$2,750,000 – 9 points
- NZ$3,000,000 – 10 points.

The applicant can be allocated additional points for accumulated earning funds that are used for direct investment funds that are invested in New Zealand to acquire a significant influence in the management of an enterprise in New Zealand (you must own at least 25% of the enterprise), and will remain in the investment for at least two years.

Points are scored as follows:

- NZ$750,000 – 3 points
- NZ$1,250,000 – 4 points
- NZ$1,750,000 – 5 points.

Points can be allocated for age. However, if you are between 55 and 64 years of age, points will be deducted as listed in the chart below. If you are 65 years of age or over, your application cannot be approved under the Business Investor Category. Points are scored as follows:

- 25-29 years of age – 10 points
- 30-34 years of age – 8 points
- 35-39 years of age – 6 points
- 40-44 years of age – 4 points
- 45-49 years of age – 2 points
- 50-54 years of age – 0 points
- 55-59 years of age – - 2 points
- 60-64 years of age – - 4 points.

Points can be awarded for settlement factors, which are those factors which will assist the applicant in settling in New Zealand.

The maximum number of points you can be awarded under this section is 7.

Settlement funds (cash, shares, stocks, and any other assets, owned wholly by the principal applicant or owned jointly by the principal applicant and spouse). A maximum of 2 points can be claimed for settlement funds, as follows:
* NZ$100,000 – 1 point
* NZ$200,000 – 2 points

Points can be awarded for your spouse's fully completed qualification, if it is comparable to a New Zealand standard. One or a series of qualifications can be considered, as follows:
* Degree, diploma or certificate of a minimum of 3 years' duration – 1 point
* Advanced qualification, master's degree or higher of a minimum of 4 years' duration – 2 points.

Points can be awarded for New Zealand business experience that you have gained in New Zealand as the owner and manager of a business, or a senior manager in a business, at the rate of 30 hours per week, or less on a pro rata basis, as follows:
* One year – 1 point
* Two years – 2 points.

Points can be allocated for family sponsorship. Your family sponsor must be over 17 years of age, residing in New Zealand, and a parent, brother, sister or child of the principal applicant or the principal applicant's spouse. Your family member is responsible for providing information about settling in New Zealand, and, if necessary, ensuring accommodation is available to you for up to 12 months from your date of arrival in New Zealand. Up to 3 points can be awarded for family sponsorship.

If you gain a points pass, you will be required to transfer your funds to New Zealand. If you were awarded points for direct investment funds, you can apply for a 12-month work visa. This allows you 12 months in which to decide on how you want to invest your funds in New Zealand. It does not allow you to enter into salaried employment in New Zealand. Once you have shown that you have made an acceptable investment, you will be granted provisional residence. You also have 12 months to transfer your settlement funds.

If you were awarded points for accumulated earnings funds but not direct investment funds, you will be given six months from the date of approval in which to transfer your funds (including investment funds). If you are determined to have made an acceptable investment of your accumulated earnings funds, you will be granted conditional residence.

Applicants must be able to score at least 11 points in the Business Investor Category to be approved.

Family Category

The aims of the Family Category are to permit New Zealand citizens or residents to be joined by their spouse or partner, and allow New Zealand citizens or residents to bring their parents, sibling, and/or child to New Zealand and help them settle. Within the Family Category, there are four sections: Partnership; Parent; Single Adult Child, Sibling, or Parent; Dependent Child.

Partnership: You can apply for residence under this section if you are:
♦ Married to and living in a genuine and stable relationship with a New Zealand citizen or resident or;
♦ Living in a genuine and stable de facto relationship of at least two years' duration with a New Zealand citizen or resident or;
♦ Living in a genuine and stable homosexual relationship of at least four years' duration with a New Zealand citizen or resident.

If you have been in a de facto relationship of at least 18 months' duration you can apply for residence, but your application will be deferred until you have been in the relationship for two years. If you have been in a homosexual relationship of at least 24 months' duration you can apply for residence, but your application will be deferred until you have been in the relationship for four years. Your relationship must be assessed as genuine and stable by the New Zealand Immigration Service before your application can be approved.

Parent: You may apply for residence under this section if you have an adult child, 17 years of age or over, who is a New Zealand citizen or resident currently residing in New Zealand who is prepared to sponsor you and:

♦ (If you have no dependent children) all of your adult children are living lawfully and permanently outside your home country or;

♦ (If you have dependent children) you have an equal or greater amount of adult children living lawfully and permanently in New Zealand than in any other single country, including your home country (referred to as "the centre of gravity principle") or;

♦ (If you have dependent children) the number of your dependent children is the same or less than the number of adult children living lawfully and permanently in New Zealand.

If your child undertakes to be your sponsor, he/she is responsible for, if necessary, ensuring that accommodation is available to you for up to 12 months from your date of arrival in New Zealand.

Single Adult Child, Brother or Sister: You may apply for residence under this section if you have a New Zealand citizen or resident parent, brother or sister or child who is prepared to sponsor you and:

♦ You are unmarried and;
♦ You have no children and;
♦ You are permanently alone in your home country.

Your family sponsor must be:

♦ 17 years of age and over and;
♦ A New Zealand citizen or resident and;

152

+ Residing in New Zealand and;
+ Your parent, brother or sister.

If your family member undertakes to be your sponsor, they are responsible for, if necessary, ensuring accommodation is available to you for up to 12 months from your date of arrival in New Zealand.

Dependent Child: You may apply for residence under this section if you are 19 years of age and:
+ You are unmarried and;
+ You have no children of your own and;
+ You are totally or substantially reliant on your parents or guardians for financial support, whether living with them or not, and;
+ Your parent or parents live lawfully and permanently in New Zealand and;
+ (If your parents are separated or divorced) custody or visitation rights of a parent living outside New Zealand would not be breached by you coming to New Zealand and;
+ (If you were born before your parents applied for residence) you were declared by your parents' application for residence or;
+ You were born after your parents applied for residence or;
+ You were adopted by your parents as a result of a New Zealand adoption or an overseas adoption recognized under New Zealand adoption law.

Humanitarian Category

This category addresses the needs of those individuals who wish to immigrate to New Zealand, where they or a close family member in New Zealand is suffering physical or emotional harm. You may apply for residence under this category if you have a close family member who is a New Zealand citizen or resident who is prepared to sponsor you and:

♦ You or a close family member is suffering serious or emotional harm and;
♦ Your circumstances are causing serious harm to you or a close family member, which can only be resolved by approving your application for residence.

Your family sponsor must be:
♦ 17 years of age and over and;
♦ A New Zealand citizen or resident and residing in New Zealand and;
♦ Your or your spouse/partner's parent, brother, sister, child, aunt, uncle, nephew, niece, grandparent or a person who has lived with and been part of your family for many years.

If your family member undertakes to be your sponsor, they are responsible for, if necessary, ensuring accommodation is available to you for up to 12 months from your date of arrival in New Zealand.

Additional Requirements

In addition to the conditions discussed above, there are other requirements of which applicants for residence in New Zealand must be aware. These include information about one's character, health, and the necessary documents proving identity and family relationships. These conditions follow:

♦ Personal documents including things such as birth, marriage, divorce, and death certificates, as well as adoption or custody papers are required.
♦ All individuals included in an application are required to be examined by the New Zealand Immigration Service and found to be in good health. Medical certificates will be required from everyone listed on the application, and x-ray certificates will be

required, except from pregnant women and children under the age of 12.

• Character Clearance — As noted in the Immigration Act, some individuals are not eligible for immigration to New Zealand. Such individuals include those who have been convicted and sentenced to prison for five years or more, or convicted and sentenced for one year or more during the last 10 years. Also, those who are considered to have ties to criminal groups or who are thought to present a danger to New Zealand or its citizens are not eligible for residency. In addition, individuals for whom arrest warrants are outstanding in any country, or people who have misrepresented themselves on their applications, are usually denied residence.

• For every applicant 17 years or older, police certificates are required.

Although New Zealand encourages immigration, it prefers that people who wish to make the country their home also bring with them skills and backgrounds that will be assets to the nation. It is true that New Zealand is open to immigrants, but it is also true that the country is selective about who in fact gains residence.

Applicants who fail to meet the requirements as listed in the Immigration Act will be denied residence. However, those who meet the requirements will be embarking on a new life that is laden with great opportunity.

After Obtaining Residence

After three years of residence, an individual living in New Zealand becomes eligible for citizenship. To gain citizenship, it is necessary to show that New Zealand has become one's genuine home. An apartment or house that is used as a legal residence is essential, as are other examples that show an individual's ties to New Zealand, including such things as steady work, ownership of a business, a driver's license, and membership in social clubs or churches. To attain citizenship, it is necessary to show that one truly considers New Zealand to be his or her home.

Chapter 16
New Zealand — Your New Home

Upon settling in New Zealand, one of your first priorities will be the establishment of a new home and entry into your community's social life. If you have children, you will register them for school, and, in all practicality, assume new routines.

Obviously, one of your first considerations will be opening an account with one of New Zealand's banks. It is likely that you will consider the Bank of New Zealand, which is one of the largest in the country. It services accounts for more than 800,000 businesses and individuals through its 300 branches. The bank also maintains branches and offices overseas in Australia, Singapore, Hong Kong, Tokyo, London, and New York.

The Bank of New Zealand is a full-service bank, handling accounts for individuals, businesses, and corporations. It also provides a full range of investment services.

The first of its services that many newcomers seek is the opening of a checking account and the procurement of a mortgage. Checking accounts are flexible, designed to meet the varying needs of consumers, while mortgages come with a variety of options. Pre-Approved Mortgage Certificates offer homebuyers the important advantage of knowing how much of a mortgage they qualify for, making it easier to purchase a home. Mortgage rates are fair and competitive. Another mortgage option is a plan called Mortgage One, in which individuals maintain all of their loans in one account. Since the consumer can access the account through checks, credit cards, or electronically, he is better able to manage his cashflow. A plan known as Check Link combines the customer's entire banking. Both loans and savings are maintained in one account, earning the customer lower costs and higher interest on deposits.

The Bank of New Zealand plays a major role in New Zealand's community life. Because it has important contacts throughout the country, it can offer newcomers significant advantages. It is well-respected, and its various branches throughout the country offer consumers the ability to bank in virtually any locale.

Other financial institutions provide a variety of services, too. The Hongkong Bank of New Zealand is another major player in finance. With more than 3,300 offices found in over 60 countries, Hongkong Bank can offer a variety of accounts, competitive rates, and an understanding of the needs and dilemmas of newcomers to New Zealand. Indeed, while it prides itself on its service to immigrants, it also offers the latest innovative services for the biggest as well as the smallest customers.

Because so many financial service centers are available, the newcomer to New Zealand is advised to shop around and set up the types of accounts that best fit his or her individual needs. There are many from which to choose.

Investing in Community and Profession

When you settle in New Zealand, you will also be entering a new community. One of the best ways to join your community is through the different leisure activities you will find.

Throughout the country, you will find opportunities to join social organizations, yacht clubs, country clubs, and church groups. By registering your children in school, you will become involved with the educational system and meet other parents. Through your new job or business, you will meet new people and find additional opportunities for leisure time, social activities.

Unquestionably, starting a business is one of the best ways to enter into the mainstream of New Zealand life. Because of the country's relatively small population, new businesses quickly establish a network of customers and clients. Moreover, you will have easy access to public officials, who, unlike those in the United States for example, are easy to contact by phone.

Many experts feel that New Zealand's climate is ripe for the start-up of new businesses, and particularly open to small businesses. Indeed, this is perhaps the greatest attraction for new-comers. Those with the experience and skills for running a business find New Zealand a marvelously invigorating environment. New Zealand is not only an excellent place to establish a proven business, but one where new ideas can often pay off big. It is one of the few business climates left where initiative and hard work can bring great success.

Along with starting a business, because of its economic growth, New Zealand needs equity finance. This area is one that offers fine opportunities for investors. There are many efficient, profitable businesses now in the country that could expand their operations and improve their prospects for growth with an infusion of equity. People with experience and management skills are also in high demand by such companies. This is especially true of those who come to New Zealand with an understanding of and contacts with businesses in their former countries. Such individuals provide New Zealand companies with enormous opportunities for overseas expansion. This fits well with the government's policy of making New Zealand a more export-driven economy. Without question, newcomers and investors are well advised to focus their capital and energies on companies that can enter this rapidly growing market.

Entrepreneurs, consultants, managers, marketing and sales personnel, investors — all of these people are in demand in New Zealand. Awaiting them are financial opportunities and the chance to live a lifestyle that few places in the world can offer.

Moving to New Zealand is not much different than moving to any other advanced country — except that New Zealanders suffer few of the problems citizens of those other lands constantly grapple with. Just as importantly, they enjoy numerous advantages.

Driving and Cars

Just about every New Zealander has access to a car. A car is almost essential to taking advantage of all the opportunities the country offers. When newcomers arrive in the country, they realize that a car is a necessity.

Motorists may choose from a large selection of cars — from the United States, Germany, and Japan. Virtually all the major models are available.

When you arrive in New Zealand, you will likely be able to use your current driver's license (from your former country), until the end of the licensing year, June 30. Thereafter, you will be required to obtain a New Zealand license. If you intend to drive to work, however, you must obtain a New Zealand license.

To obtain a New Zealand driver's license, you must pass a test on theory. The testing procedure varies, based on the country in which you hold your original license. To find out more specific information, you should check with the License Testing Office.

Final Reflections

New Zealand offers myriad opportunities for investors and immigrants. Whereas much of the rest of the advanced world seems to be in decline, both economically and spiritually, New Zealand offers a safe haven, a place that embodies new, exciting, and wonderful options. Just consider:

+ There are business and investment opportunities in New Zealand that few other countries can match.
+ New Zealand offers a friendly atmosphere and unhurried lifestyle.
+ In New Zealand you will enjoy clean air in a generally pollution-free environment.
+ New Zealand offers a high standard of living.

◆ New Zealand offers many people the qualities of life they can no longer find in their present countries.

Without doubt, migrating to New Zealand provides people with opportunities that they may never realize in their former countries. You owe yourself this chance to make New Zealand your home and achieve all the wonderful advantages and benefits of living in the Land of Kiwis.

Hiking in the Southern Alps.

Appendix

Following is a list of potentially helpful contacts. While the author does not endorse any individuals or companies listed below, they are presented as good starting points should you seek the specific information or services they provide. Note that although many of the following maintain offices in various New Zealand cities, in most cases only the address and phone numbers of the Auckland offices have been provided. You can easily obtain information regarding regional offices by contacting the main office.

Immigration Consultants

You might wish to contact the following, compare their offers, and then make your selection if you feel that a consultant service will be helpful to you.

A.I.C. Immigration Consultancy, Ltd.
3rd Floor, Dilworth Building
Cnr Queen and Customs Sts.
Auckland 1, New Zealand
Phone: 64-9-302-2091
Fax: 64-9-302-2096

ANZ
Cnr Queen & Victoria Sts.
P.O. Box 62
Auckland, New Zealand
Phone: 0-9-358-9200
Fax: 0-9-358-5280

ASB Bank
Immigration and Financial Advisory Division
ASB Building, Cnr Queen and Wellesley Sts.
Auckland, New Zealand
Phone: 64-9-377-8930
Fax: 64-9-302-1815

H.S. Golian Immigration and Investment
Campbell House, 11 Campbell Rd
P.O. Box 24342 Royal Oak.
Auckland, New Zealand
Phone: 64-9-624-1204
Fax: 64-9-624-3645

Integrity Immigration Service
P.O. Box 9912, Newmarket
Auckland, New Zealand
Phone: 64-9-524-2814
Fax: 64-9-525-9010

International Migration Services, Ltd.
17B Parkway Dr.
Mairangi Bay, Auckland 10
PO Box 101162
North Shore Mail Centre
Auckland, New Zealand
Phone: 0-9-479-6886
Fax: 0-9-479-7205

Legget Immigration Consultants
2 Whitaker Place, Symonds St.
P.O. Box 5568
Auckland, New Zealand
Phone: 64-9-303-4660
Fax: 64-9-303-1572

Malcolm Pacific, Ltd.
5th Floor, 70 Symonds St.
Auckland, New Zealand
Phone: 64-9-309-4187
Fax: 64-9-366-4730

Southern Skies Consultants
9/158 Beach Rd., Parnell
Auckland, New Zealand
Phone: 0-64-9-303-1412
Fax: 0-64-9-303-1414

Banks

ASB Bank
Manager, Migrant Banking Division
First Floor, ASB Building
Cnr Queen and Wellesley Sts.
Auckland, New Zealand
Phone: 09-377-8930
Fax: 09-302-1815

ANZ Bank
Migrant Services Unit
ANZ House, Level Six
Cnr Queen & Victoria Sts., Auckland 1
P.O. Box 62
Auckland, New Zealand
Phone: 0-9-358-9200
Fax: 0-9-358-5280

166

Bank of New Zealand
Auckland Branch
P.O. Box 13
80 Queen St.
Auckland, New Zealand
Phone: 0-9-375-1300
Fax: 0-9-375-1301

Hongkong Bank
P.O. Box 5947
Hongkong Bank House
290 Queen St.
Auckland, New Zealand
Phone: 09-309-3800
Fax: 09-309-6681

Attorneys

In New Zealand, attorneys are known as barristers. Following are some firms. Note that these firms often provide a variety of services to immigrants, including help with migration requirements, company acquisition, company start-ups, investment opportunities, and property-related services.

Bell, Bully, Buddle, Weir
Auckland, New Zealand
Phone: 64-9-309-0859
Fax: 64-9-309-3312

Glaister Enno
18 High St.
P.O. Box 63
Auckland, New Zealand
Phone: 64-9-307-8243
Fax: 64-9-303-4320

Lane, Neave, Ronaldson
119 Armagh St.
P.O. Box 13-149
Christchurch, New Zealand
Phone: 64-3-379-3720
Fax: 64-3-379-8370

The Fortune Manning Law Partnership
Price Waterhouse Centre
66 Wyndham St.
P.O. Box 4139
Auckland 1, New Zealand
Phone: 64-9-309-0246
Fax: 64-9-309-0573

Simpson, Grierson, Butler, White
Simpson Grierson Building
92-96 Albert St.
Private Bag 92 518, Wellesley St.
Auckland, New Zealand
Phone: 64-9-358-2222
Fax: 64-9-307-0331

If you are interested in information on news and jobs in New Zealand, you would be well advised to subscribe to *New Zealand News UK.* The paper is international in scope, being read in 66 countries, and offers a regular immigrant section that details business opportunities, employment, real estate, and education in articles that provide valuable information for those considering moving to New Zealand. Contact: Circulation Manager, New Zealand News UK, P.O. Box 10, Berwick-Upon-Tweed, Northumberland, TD15 IBW, UK.

New Zealand News UK

YOU WILL ALSO WANT TO READ:

☐ **10059 PERSONAL PRIVACY THROUGH FOREIGN INVESTING,** *by Trent Sands.* If you're frustrated with all the paperwork and taxes that burden the American investor, let Trent Sands show you how to safely and secretly move your dollars overseas. This book shows how to research foreign investment markets and set up an overseas bank account. Covers: Switzerland, The Bahamas, The Cayman Islands, Bermuda, Great Britain, Australia, New Zealand, Luxembourg, Canada and more. A world of opportunities for the privacy-conscious investor. *1993, 5½ x 8½, 72 pp, soft cover.* **$10.00.**

☐ **61147 HOW TO LEGALLY OBTAIN A SECOND CITIZENSHIP AND PASSPORT — AND WHY YOU WANT TO,** *by Adam Starchild.* An American citizenship and passport are two of the most highly prized possessions a person can have... but there are distinct legal and financial advantages to having a second citizenship and passport. Author Adam Starchild explains the reasons and methods for acquiring both, in high highly informative book. Covered are: A brief history of passports and nationality; How nationality is acquired; The advantages and disadvantages of multiple nationalities; How a second passport is obtained; Prerequisites for acquiring both a second citizenship and passport. *1995, 5½ x 8½, 131 pp, soft cover.* **$15.00.**

☐ **17084 I WALKED AWAY, An Expatriate's Guide to Living Cheaply in Thailand,** *by Michael Zeising.* Ready to take a permanent vacation... *in Thailand?* Michael Zeising was, and he chronicles his experience in this informative display of his thought process and day-to-day living tips. Zeising discusses how he came to his decision to leave the United States, how he divested himself of the many material objects that were holding him back, and how he chose his destination. This is the most explicit, helpful book ever written for fledgling expatriates. *1996, 5½ x 8½, 147 pp, illustrated, soft cover.* **$14.95.**

☐ **17079 TRAVEL-TRAILER HOMESTEADING UNDER $5,000,** *by Brian Kelling.* Tired of paying rent? Need privacy away from nosy neighbors? This book will show how a modest financial investment can enable you to place a travel-trailer or other RV on a suitable piece of land and make necessary improvements for a comfortable home in which to live! This book covers the cost break-down, tools needed, how to select the land and travel-trailer or RV, and how to install a septic system, as well as water, power (including solar panels), heat and refrigeration systems. Introduction by Bill Kaysing. *1995, 5½ x 8½, 80 pp, illustrated, indexed, soft cover.* **$8.00**

Loompanics Unlimited
PO Box 1197
Port Townsend, WA 98368

NZG7

Please send me the books I have checked above. I have enclosed $_____ which includes $4.95 for shipping and handling of the first $20.00 ordered. Add an additional $1 shipping for each additional $20 ordered. Washington residents include 7.9% sales tax.

Name_____

Address _____

City/State/Zip _____

VISA and MasterCard accepted. 1-800-380-2230 for credit card orders *only.*
8am to 4pm, PST, Monday through Friday.